Winter Tales
Men Write about Aging

Winter Tales

Men Write about Aging

edited by

Duff Brenna
and
Thomas E. Kennedy

SERVING HOUSE BOOKS

ISBN: 978-0-9838289-0-7

Cover photo of George Washington Cable from The Library of Congress

Serving House Books logo by Barry Lereng Wilmont

Published by Serving House Books, LLC
Copenhagen and Florham Park, NJ

www.servinghousebooks.com

First Serving House Books Edition 2011

To the memory of Norman Mailer

Table of Contents

Winter Tales:
An Introduction

Up to a point it isn't so bad this aging thing. But ultimately annoying cruelties start pestering your body, perhaps even your mind. Maybe it's your knees. Maybe it's your back. Maybe it's that walnut gripping your urethra, the infamous prostate. Maybe it's your hair falling out. Or your teeth. Maybe you're getting more forgetful than usual. You can't recall people's names. The memory ain't what she used to be, old man. Where are your keys? Where's your wallet? What movie did you watch on TV last night?

To counterbalance the gray hair you see sprouting, you start coloring it. If you have a mustache and/or beard, you get your youth back by using a product called JUST FOR MEN. You grow a pony tail to compensate for your receding hairline. You start using face creams to soften and blur the crow's feet invading the orbs around your eyes. There are more doctor visitations. More prescriptions for blood pressure, high cholesterol, anxiety, impotence. It's curious to note the person you're becoming, the furrowed brow, the aches and pains, the troubles of a body slowly declining in a world that is still wonderful, still full of bittersweet moments you cherish. You don't look at all youthful anymore, but inside your head you're still eighteen. Well, maybe twenty. Twenty-five?

Around you, there are people, perhaps loved ones, beginning to depart. You fall back on the rewards of memory which keep him or her alive inside you. The days are dimming. The nights are longer. You find it hard to sleep. Your sexual energy is furtive and uncertain at best.

What is one to do in the midst of such difficulties? Maybe follow the dictum St. Augustine of Hippo was given when he was told to "take and read"? Only in this case, instead of scriptures, you open an anthology filled with writers dealing with certain adjustments in their lives that you are dealing with too. You "take and read" a book called *Winter Tales* and recognize the comforting fact that there is a large brotherhood of aging males, many of whom seem to speak for you, your experiences mirrored in theirs.

The first offering you peruse is an interview conducted by Michael Lee, a riveting conversation with Norman Mailer who talks about some of the authors he has known, Ernest Hemingway, John Cheever, F. Scott Fitzgerald and others. He tells us how hard it is to call up words that used to come easily to him when he was writing. Nowadays words seem to be hiding from his aging brain. This was Mailer's last interview conducted six months before he died. The interview is filled with open and honest revelations, a calm, reflective Mailer who is easy to sympathize with and even love, especially now that he's gone to that Great Perhaps. Perchance Elysium, the Isle of the Blessed? We can hope so.

Robert Pinsky writes amusingly about how forgetful he is and how it will happen to the young who think somehow their memories are immortal: "You'll see, you little young jerks: your favorite music and your political/ Furors, too, will need to get sorted in dusty electronic corridors." Gordon Weaver creates a litany of his body's failures and tells us jealously that "Women, by custom, may and do retard or mitigate such evidence in their vanity's glass—dyes and moisturizing lotions, cosmetics and cosmetic surgeries, chemical injections. But male pride, also by custom, requires a stoic survey of the evidences of the ravages of Time." It's an essay filled with naked honesty and dark humor written in the style and language of a master wordsmith.

Billy Collins writes a humorous song about going bald. Stephen Dunn describes what it was like to turn 50 and then 60.

Thomas E. Kennedy writes a raucous, but also serious essay about a prostate cancer scare he had a few years ago. At the 2008 National Magazine Awards, Kennedy's essay written for the *Winter Tales* project, "I am Joe's Prostate," won first prize, the Ellie. His essay, printed in *New Letters*, was chosen over Stephen King and essays from *The New Yorker, Harper's,* and *The Atlantic.* James Brown writes about what it was like to take steroids, how he loved what steroids and weightlifting did to his aging body, but definitely did not love what happened to his brain, his treacherous mind.

Robert Gover motors through his life identified by the many cars he's owned over the years. Steve Heller tells us what it is like being married to a much younger woman and trying to keep up with her by taking up a new sport—rollerblading. Walter Cummins contemplates the possibility of an afterlife. Jack Marshall confesses that his aging face is covering a child's heart. Albert Goldbarth gives us a history lesson, taking us back to the Revolutionary War and mixing it with the present, using metaphor to tell us wisely about life: *Love every stitch. Remember every thread.*

Steve Davenport roils a rhyme at Coffee Joe's league night 55-and-over. Joseph Millar lays out the truth about broken marriages, raising kids while age is slowing you down making it impossible to work the way you used to. Nicholas Birns mourns the death of his heroes, great athletes who meant so much to him, but now remind him of his own mortality. Sam Hamod writes a love letter to the dear departed Lorca, Neruda, and Borges. Victor Rangel-Ribeiro has intimations of immortality. Greg Herriges reflects on the life of his younger brother who died of full-blown AIDS. Steve Kowit reminds us of how unpredictable and often surprising death can be. Lennox Raphael sees the immortality of art as a revenge against time and that there is a certain qualified "joy" in aging. Paul Casey describes with humor and angst his colonoscopy. Liam Mac Sheóinín muses on the literary preoccupations possessed by graying genius, diabetes and a tricky heart. George Dickerson tells us how to take "a jaunty, jocular leave." Dave Poe lays down everything we need to know about the good life versus pancreatitis. Michael Begnal speaks about alcohol, anxiety and aging.

An appropriate thematic touch is given to us in an offering by Nobel Prize Winner Mario Vargas Llosa who writes with great humor about young athletes and sports and how his alter ego in *The Notebooks of Don Rigoberto* has come to hate them all and how jealous he is that his body will no longer respond with the kind of energy it used to have when he was younger and lustful. Speaking to athletes in general he says: "Yes, it's true, in your atrophied intellect a light has come on: I consider the practice of sports in general, and the cult of sports in particular, as radical forms of the imbecility that brings human beings close to sheep, geese, and ants, three extreme examples of animal gregariousness."

Jack Driscoll remembers an actual athlete, strongman Charles Atlas, what an inspiration he was before he died at 79. Niels Hav leaves us with his dark, comic "Encouragement."

And so it goes—on and on, a miscellaneous abundance shimmering with life in illustrations by James Campbell and in poems and essays filled with insight, wisdom and humor, riveting accounts that will make you sad, make you happy, perhaps even giddy, perhaps wiser, and certainly contemplative, make you see yourself and others you know who are in the same predicament. You may find yourself smiling wryly and even laughing at times. This is a bright book of life, not death, which these wonderful (at times brilliant) artists have created. We are certain it is a timely book, given our country's aging population of boomers who will take comfort in knowing they are not alone when it comes to dealing with what aging is doing to their minds and bodies. With lots of love and understanding, the Winter Tales writers reach out to us, telling us that we may all be in the same boat as it drifts downstream carrying a world of humanity towards an uncertain but inevitable rendezvous, but as George Dickerson says in "Badinage for 'Pepper'" "... screw the wizard of finality." Amen and Hoo-Haw! Take and read. Join the camaraderie. Welcome aboard, dear agers.

Duff Brenna — 2011

Norman Mailer & Michael Lee
(the last interview)

Please Do Not Understand Me Too Quickly

I think I know myself pretty well by now and there's really not much use for regrets. What I did well was because I had the luck to have the background that would enable me to do well. And what I did poorly are mostly things I've tried to overcome in my life and generally ended up with mixed returns.

—Norman Mailer

He might move a little slower and with some discomfort these days from the pain in his arthritic knees, and yet, sitting on the porch across from Norman Mailer on a salty, windswept day, he seemed virtually unchanged since the first time I sat with him close to 25 years ago in the same spot. He's funny, challenging, competitive, opinionated, and dauntingly smart. And no matter who's doing the slicing or how severely, Norman Mailer remains one of the most important literary figures of modern times. Born on January 31, 1923, the Mailer oeuvre includes 32 books, a volume of poetry, a drama, numerous films both as actor and director and countless awards and honors including two Pulitzer Prizes.

Lee: It's been 53 years since the publication of *The Naked and the Dead*, and this is sort of a "where were you when Jack Kennedy was shot" question, but do you remember the exact moment you heard your first novel was going to be published?

Mailer: You know, it never had an exact moment, really. There was a history to it. It went first to Little, Brown because my sister had a good friend she'd known at Radcliff that was working at Little, Brown—youngest editor they ever had too, 22 years old. I showed her the first two hundred pages and she wrote a rave report and said this is going to be *the* war novel of World War II and the upper people at Little, Brown said, oh here's this college kid and she's friends with the family. Anyway, they read it and got upset because there were so many "fugs" in it. I had to use "fug" instead of "fuck," which was the only thing you could do in those days. Using the word fuck was hopeless at that point until James Jones came along in 1951 with "f-u-c-k" and then it worked. Now you can't write a decent American sentence without three fucks in it. So they read it and were very worried about the number of fugs. It finally got published with about three quarter of the number of fugs, which was enough. But I didn't really believe it was going to be published until I saw the book in my hand.

Lee: Do you ever go back and reread your work?

Mailer: Not that much because I find it's one place where feedback is no good. You get too taken up with yourself in the past, old triumphs and old defeats come back, so unless you're going to write a book about yourself it isn't a good idea.

Lee: When I read some of my old stories, I cringe at the lack of craftsmanship and wisdom. But there is an energy there, a kind of exuberance of the language that I'm not sure I always match today. I don't notice that drop off of energy in your work and I'm wondering if that's a conscious effort on your part?
 Mailer: You've probably had problems I haven't had, among other

things, in that I had one piece of great luck that I didn't realize was great luck in the beginning, which was this: ever since *The Naked and the Dead* came out I've not had to work for a living. I've worked as a writer and haven't had to do other jobs over that time. And jobs undercut your energy. Even the best of jobs has a lot of sludge in it, and this sludge erodes style. And I'm sure you know—I've never known a young writer who didn't have that bitterness that creeps in at the way they can't use their time properly. And for years, I used to think, oh shit, I've been cut off from life, I'm too successful too early and the only way you really learn anything is on a job, which is also true. But of course I had one job for two years and that was the Army and that gave me a hell of a lot of real experiences as opposed to experience you search for, which is always the problem for young writers. If they don't have enough experience, they search for it, and that always has a lifeline to it—you can get out of it. It's the situations you can't get out of that really give you the kind of knowledge you want as a writer. In a certain sense, existential experience is usually dramatic, you know, you get in a terrible skid on a snowy road and you're either going to come out of it alive or broken or safe. So you have a moment that's existential, that's intense. But there's also slow existential experience which is getting into a situation at work where this may be what you do the rest of your life and you don't want to do it. That slow existential experience is valuable for writing, but it takes so long. And so I think a lot of one's good style can get chewed up through going through the grind and stone of daily work. To finish my point, I used to feel that I didn't know anything because I got too rich too soon. I used to feel sorry for myself, but now I look back and I'm uneasy about those feelings because the truth is I had the time to store things and use a certain amount of leisure.

Lee: You were very vocal about your opposition to the Vietnam War, in fact, went to jail over it. How did your experiences in the Army as a rifleman in a reconnaissance platoon inform your writing—not so much in *The Naked and the Dead*, but how it helped formulate who you were then and are now? And do you think you would have felt differently about Vietnam had you been a nineteen-year-old rifleman patrolling the outskirts of Khe Sanh in Vietnam instead of Manila?

Mailer: No question I would have felt differently. You have to. But I'm not sure I would have ended up saying that war had to be fought either. Listen, there was more justification for World War II, but I used to hate that war. I used to feel it was idiocy. I think I probably would have been the same way at Khe Sanh. I remember in the war I was in, which was in the Pacific, it was hard to believe in the Japs as a terrible, terrible enemy, because the only Japanese we saw were dead or people coming in as prisoners who were emaciated and it was obvious they were hurting badly. And they were smaller than us, physically speaking, so there was a feeling, finally, who were we fighting and why? And then of course at the end with the atom bomb, on one hand we all felt very happy the war was going to be over and we were going home, but the impact of it didn't hit us until years later. Now they talk about the Great War and the great generation and there wasn't much of that feeling around then. We didn't even have much fun compared to the guys in Europe who could at least hit Paris. Manila was not Paris.

Lee: So it didn't impact your life much beyond that experience?

Mailer: No, it had an impact in other ways. It had some very good effects; it left me permanently modest, because if you're working with a guy who's illiterate and he can dig a sump hole or anything better than you can, that reminds you that you're not as good as you think you are. And there was an awful lot of that. I used to rate myself if there were fifteen men left in a platoon, I'd be somewhere about fifth, or sixth—maybe seventh—from the bottom. I wouldn't be fifth best. So when I came out of that war, what it kept in me forever was a certain sense of staying away from judgments and stay away from superiority with your characters. And I think if there's one merit to my work it's that I don't trash my characters which most novelists will do because it's an easy way to settle a lot of old grudges.

Lee: Let's dabble a bit into politics. How different do you think this country would be if Bobby Kennedy had his eight years?

Mailer: All I know is that if Bobby Kennedy had not been assassinated and won the election, we would have had a totally different country. But how it would have gone, I don't know. I've gotten old enough to realize that just because something starts well doesn't mean it will end well. I think it would have been a better country and a more interesting country because I think there was something fine with him and special.

Lee: Did you know him?

Mailer: Slightly. I met him once.

Lee: I talked to George Plimpton about Bobby Kennedy (he roomed with him at Harvard and was in that kitchen in California with him when he was killed) and he said there were two Bobby's—the good one and the very bad one. Plimpton said that as Bobby got older, the good one really emerged.

Mailer: Well I described him once without having met him, saying that he had a look on his face—I saw him at conventions and things— and what I used was house football at Harvard as an example. I said that you would get one glint of recognition as you faced off against him on the line, but the moment the ball was passed, there would be a knee in your groin. [laughs] When I met him he said something about, "You're a mean man with a word, Mr. Mailer." Anyway, I saw a not bad Bobby, but a difficult one because it was at the time he defeated Eugene McCarthy and I wanted to know why they didn't get along. It was my argument that they were essentially splitting their strength. And he started throwing terms at me like, "What about H.R. number 1246?" I didn't know what it meant then and I don't know what it means now, but he'd say "What about that one, eh Mailer?"

Lee: That's a nasty way to argue.

Mailer: Yeah, and we got nowhere. And then at the very end he turned gentle for a moment and he said, "Well, really, you might as well vote for McCarthy—he's your man." And I told him, no, I was going to vote for him.

Lee: Would you respond to a few quotes attributed to you? You once said, "Violence is the last frontier of literature."

Mailer: Well, that's simple enough, it's just that we've categorized so much and violence is hard to write about well. Anyone who's ever been in any kind of violence at all knows all the peculiar phenomena associated with it, the odd detachment that's present in violence, the way time slows down. The movies try to capture that occasionally by slowing the camera down, but it's the sense that you are in another place—the intense existential quality of it. So I didn't mean, oh let's all get violent so we can write good literature because after all, anyone who goes seeking for violence is in another category altogether. But if violence comes upon you, I've always found that—in the few times in my life when I've been associated with violence in a real way—it stays with me forever and it is a source of writing. See, I have a theory on writing that I've expressed from time to time, but it might be worth telling you again. I think that there are certain experiences that I speak of as crystals and they're the ones you shouldn't write about. For instance, I've never written about my childhood mainly because my feeling is that too many crystals are there and the value of a crystal is that you can beam your imagination through this crystal in one direction and end up with one or another scenario. Even from another direction, you get a different scenario from the same crystal. So you don't want to write about the material that's in the crystal. Preserve it because it's endlessly fruitful for you. And I'd say in a funny, crazy way, even though sex has been written about in a hundred different ways and trod over like a field of bulldozers have gone over a few choice acres and left it all mired, nonetheless, it's still very hard to write about sex well and say something new. Anything that goes to the root is worth writing about but of course the whole process of modern society is to alienate us from the roots.

Lee: We've talked on occasion about Hemingway and I always felt I understood his suicide. Forget that suicide ran in his family. The one thing that mattered to him — his writing — had been taken away by what might have been Alzheimer's or whatever.

Mailer: He would have been awfully young for that.

Lee: I see a contentment about you now that I don't think Hemingway ever had.

Mailer: Well, you know he overextended himself. He had a lot of balls, there's just no getting around it. And the balls were to take real chances with his life. I'm not just talking about the things he did in terms of physical feats. Physically speaking, I think he was a braver man than I am, but I don't think he was, like, five times braver than me — I think he was twenty-five or thirty per cent braver. Because to me, bravery has also been very important over the years when I've tried things. But I think he was truly overextended because he came from a mid-western family that was only partially cultured. And now here he was, one of the intellectual leaders of the world, willy-nilly. He didn't ask to be an intellectual leader, but he was seen that way. Every one of his pronouncements had a papal ring to them, especially for young writers where he had enormous influence. And I think for him, he was immensely obsessed with death all the time. And I do think his father's suicide was a prodigious part of that. I remember there was a talented, young writer here, whose name I don't recall, who died in a motorcycle accident. But he had said in an interview that he was thinking of committing suicide, but he knew he couldn't do it because if you commit suicide, you condemn your sons to suicide.

Lee: Was that John Gardner, maybe?

Mailer: Exactly. Yeah. And I thought that was an amazing remark and quite true and I thought he was thinking of Hemingway. But anyway, what I'm getting at, I'm not so sure Hemingway committed suicide. I have this theory that every night, whenever he was feeling truly sick and bad, he would take a shotgun, load it, and put the muzzle in his mouth, reach down with his thumb and play with the trigger. He certainly knew where to cross the barrier.

Lee: Let's just talk a little about aging. Do you feel more captive by it now and what its day-to-day realities are as opposed to, say, when we sat down for our interview five years ago?

Mailer: Oh yeah. Well your physical limitations move in. It's like a tide that comes in. And your incapacities move in. In other words, I take it for granted that I'm never going to be traveling through a wonderful foreign city in Italy, let's say, exploring it. That's gone forever. Walking is difficult. I don't enjoy walking. I force myself to walk a couple hundred yards a day. So in that sense — of course the cartilage is gone in my knees.

Lee: Is it just because you didn't want to undergo the recuperative process to have your knees replaced?

Mailer: I'm too old for it. The knees went bad about five years ago and at that point, the doctor said, well we can certainly do it, but I'm not going to do them both at once. I'll do them one at a time.

Lee: That's a year.

Mailer: That's a year. And I thought I'm too old for that. If I knew I had ten years, okay, I'd do it. But what if I pop off in two years and I've lost one of them to this? And I can live with it, it's not that bad. It isn't like I live in pain and can't sleep at night. It's just tough to walk. So that's one thing. My hearing is going and my teeth. By the way, make sure you don't have any infected teeth if you go through a heart operation or they'll take out your teeth.

Lee: Really?

Mailer: Well, what's the definition of a doctor? He's a human biped who covers his buttocks.

Lee: Has aging impacted your writing process?

Mailer: No, I don't think so.

Lee: Do you have more big novels in you?

Mailer: I don't know, I hope so. The point is, one of the things that happens when you get older is your command of your vocabulary begins to diminish. Very slowly, but it does. And you never know when your brain is going to give out on you. My knees have given out on me, my ears have given out, my teeth now. So, I don't feel any certainty at all that I've got another big novel in me. I'm going to write it. I have it in my mind and in my sentiments, but whether I'll be physically able to do it, to go through the grind of two or three very tough years is something I just can't predict.

Lee: Do you think much about death?

Mailer: No. Surprisingly, not that much. I've thought about it all my life, so — I really feel death is the beginning of another existence. I believe in karma, I believe we're reincarnated.

Lee: In a human form?

Mailer: Well, that's not knowable. Listen, I've seen so many dogs that are more human than humans, that I'm not so sure — it may be the nearest we come to heaven is to be reborn as dogs. I mean the love a dog feels. How often do we feel that much love for anything?

Lee: You also once said about fears, "I fear decrepitude."

Mailer: Yeah, now I'm getting on the edge of that. [laughs] I don't fear it now. It's very interesting. What I've discovered about growing old is that there are a few tricks to it, well not tricks, but benefits. And one of them is that when I walk my knees hurt. On the other hand, since I'm a great believer in karma, I figure that's as close as we ever get to heaven or hell, is that when we're reborn, the hellish part of the new life is where you are paying for your sins, so to speak, and the happy part of the new life is the nearest you're ever going to get to heaven. You're rewarded for your good deeds. It's a rather tidy little system. But anyway, when I'm walking and feeling pain in the knees, I feel pretty good about it because I feel like I'm paying off my bad karma on the installment plan. The one thing you don't want to lose is your mind. The senses all begin to go.

Lee: Is there a sadness as you get older? You're burying friends. . .

Mailer: No. There are regrets. On the other hand, I think I know myself pretty well by now and there's really not much use for regrets. What I did well was because I had the luck to have the background that would enable me to do well. And what I did poorly are mostly things I've tried to overcome in my life and generally ended up with mixed returns. I always wanted to be a real good boxer and worked hard at it, but never got that good. On the other hand, now that I look back on it, I think, well, not that bad. I was about as good a boxer as I was a skier—a confirmed mediocre.

Lee: Let's talk briefly about the writing process. Do you still work as hard as you used to? What's your writing day like?

Mailer: No, I used to be able to put in long, long days. Now about two hours in the morning and two hours in the afternoon are about it. And it takes me all day to do those two hours, in other words, a lot of time is wasted getting into it and the time in between takes longer. But you know you don't have to be able to write more than a couple hours a day in order to get a book done in a year. A short book; my trouble is I don't write short books.

Lee: Do you establish a daily word quota?

Mailer: No, because so much depends on how hard the particular passage is that you're working on. You can spend a day and feel virtuous at the end of it if you've done two or three pages. And then you have days when you do ten pages.

Lee: Do you ever show any of your unfinished work to anyone?

Mailer: Very rarely, but I will sometimes.

Lee: Do you get to read any of your contemporaries?

Mailer: A little bit, but not much. They've got this old saying that if you're working on a book it's like a guy taking your car apart and all the parts are on the floor of the garage and this Ferrari roars by. So I don't like to read too good a book when I'm working because it brings out my competitiveness and it also brings out my sense of frustration—there are my parts on the floor. One thing that I've said over and over, but worth saying again, I think, what's not understood about good writers is that they're as competitive as athletes. And so when I read a good book, I don't read it the way other people do. I don't read it to go through a profound experience, I read it critically, the way one athlete will watch another's performance. Not watch it with venom, quite the contrary, watch it very competitively. You might say to yourself, his spiral is tighter than mine and he's got about five yards on me at least, maybe ten on a long pass, but on the other hand, he's more lead-footed than I am. And the whole thing when you're reading a good novel is to give it its credit and not try to smudge over its good parts by saying the guy's overrated. What you want to do is say, the guy's overrated here and better than I am there, and that's the way I read. It churns me up because then I want to write about the book. I think if I had my druthers, I could end up a critic in a funny way, because I know so much about novel writing by now. I can always tell when a guy is writing out of his best vein and when he's faking it. Whenever you write a novel, your knowledge is not going to be equal over all the aspects of it—not that the novel has any variety to it—I mean some of the best novels have been written out of one vein and one only. But you have to be able to look at something like *The Great Gatsby* and say that when all is said and done, Fitzgerald didn't know *anything* about gangsters. And what made the book so wonderful is that Americans didn't know anything about gangsters either at that point, and so a myth was born of Gatsby. But you could go through a hundred thousand gangsters before you found one Gatsby, even the ones of late.

Lee: That might be my favorite American novel.

Mailer: Really? It's so full of shit. But it's a lovely book, it's beautifully written.

Lee: How about a few opinions of some writers? John Cheever?

Mailer: By the way, that I never do. I'll do it for Cheever for special reasons, but I don't do that because it's a very expensive way to live in that you can say something off the top of your head and then the particular writer will never forgive you. Quite rightly.

Lee: I had all dead guys in mind.

Mailer: These are all dead people? All right, then I can talk. [laughs] Cheever's funny. I never read him when he was alive—hardly read him—I considered him a spoiled New Yorker darling and we didn't like each other much the few times we met and we had slightly disagreeable set-to's. Nothing dramatic, but just didn't like each other too much. And then toward the end of his life he read *The Executioner's Song* and wrote a good review of it, which mollified me. And then I started reading his short stories after he died. They were wonderful, they were extraordinary. I don't think I enjoyed a book of short stories as much—I think I'd have to go to Chekov before I could come up with stories I enjoyed more. And so I just felt rueful, rueful that I never read him while he was alive and how much better he was than I thought he was. And what a loss, we could have had a good conversation or two instead of a couple of dull ones, holding each other at arm's length. Who's next?

Lee: Let's go back to Hemingway.

Mailer: Hemingway. Oh, that's a book. For years I wanted to do a biography of Hemingway and finally gave up on it because I figured it would take too much of my life. I think he was maybe the narrowest literary genius who ever lived, but he was a genius. There were times when I think, well, he's very good but let's not get carried away. I remember after I wrote *The Executioner's Song*, which expressed my own sense of humor about literary style because everyone was saying for years, "Oh Mailer's so baroque and he just can't write simply," and there was a vogue on those years honoring all those who could write simply. There was a period where the minimalists were doing something and I thought writing simply is much easier than writing complexly and I'll show it. And I wrote *Executioner's Song*, which after all is a pretty good book written in a very simple style. So after I finished I thought, let me take a look at Hemingway because there's nothing to writing simply. And then I read Hemingway and I realized, no, no, no. No, the style of *Executioner's Song* doesn't begin to compare to Hemingway's style. I think I was reading *A Moveable Feast*, where maybe his style was more sophisticated than anywhere else. And so what I felt was no, he's a great writer, absolutely great, and he has done more with a simple sentence than anyone who ever lived. Anyone. I don't care what nationality.

Lee: Just one other. Eddie Bonetti.

Mailer: Bonetti? Eddie could have been a major writer, certainly a major short story writer, if he hadn't been so spooked. Writing was just too damned difficult for him. I've known one other person who was a particularly dear friend of mine, Jean Malaquais, who would work with huge pain. He'd write fourteen hours a day and come up with two or three hundred words; a brilliant man. And I said to him once, why do you work that hard? Because he was very unsuccessful—he published, but couldn't make a living writing. I said, you have so much on the ball and could make a living in so many other ways, why do you write? He said, oh no, I could never give it up because the only time I know something is true is when I find it at the point of my pen. And I thought about that for years, because there is that wonderful feeling of truth you get. Well, Eddie was always finding truth at the point of his pen and then there was such wars that always went on in Eddie that then the other side of him would then attack the truth he found. And he'd have to rework it. And rework it, and rework it. He felt such an awe about writing, he really felt almost like a primitive who danced to do a drawing on the cave and what will happen when the ghost of that animal that was drawn comes back to attack him? Eddie was absolutely spooked by the huge consequences of writing, that you're interfering with the gods and the devils and the spirits. You had to ameliorate them, you had to make peace with them, you had to go to war with them. And he used all his energy in side contests. And he rewrote too much. His inner nature was like that. He could have been a major writer if he hadn't had all those obstacles within.

Lee: He would obsess over a paragraph and never continue until that paragraph was finished.

Mailer: Yeah. Well remember with his car? I got that image of the car with the parts all out on the floor through Eddie. You know, then he'd put the motor together again and there'd be one little sound and he was such a perfectionist that he destroyed his larger possibilities.

Lee: I remember Eddie telling me one time when he was in the New England Golden Gloves as a flyweight and he'd just beaten some kid and he looked down at his father sitting ringside. His father just shook his head, disgusted with his performance. And Eddie said, "I knew I could never please that old bastard. Ever."

Mailer: He never told me that.

Lee: And I wonder how much of that carried into other areas of Eddie's life.

Mailer: I think you've got something there. Eddie is one of those writers who saw God as the ultimate critic and so if God is your ultimate critic, then you really have to rework what you're doing. And I must say, he didn't often ruin stuff he worked on all that hard; it ended up being very, very good. *The Wine Cellar* is a wonderful book. I'll tell you one story about Eddie that maybe you haven't heard. Did you ever hear about the night he was going to kill Anatole Broyard? [laughs]

Lee: From a bad review of *The Wine Cellar*?

Mailer: Yeah. Well, what happened was Broyard had written a review for *The Times* that spoke of how here's this author who really doesn't amount to much whose been picked up by people like Jackie Kennedy and Richard Goodwin and Norman Mailer, and they all tout him. And so he gets published but this book is really not worth anything. Well, of course, if Eddie had a thought that was eating at the very pit of his soul's foundation, it was, what if this is true? If it's true I have to kill someone or kill myself. [laughs] It was a point of the deepest honor. So he came to my house one night about midnight and said, [a growly impersonation] "Norman, can we talk? I'm going to go kill Anatole Broyard. I heard he's down in Newport and I know where he is. I'm going to get in my truck now and go kill him." And I said, "Oh, Eddie, for Christ's sakes, you can't kill him. It isn't worth destroying yourself for that son of a bitch. He's just bitter." Well, we talked for about two or three hours and finally I didn't talk him out of it as much as I wore him out of it. So by three in the morning, and sodden with booze, he no longer felt like going

30

all the way to Newport. So he never killed Anatole Broyard, but he would have, I think. But I always felt afterward, well, you know Eddie died about ten years after that of that cancer, and I always felt maybe I made a mistake. Maybe I should have let him go kill Anatole Broyard. [laughs]

Lee: If I'm not mistaken he stalked Benjamin DeMott for a few weeks because of a bad review.

Mailer: You know something interesting, I received a dreadful review from DeMott on *Ancient Evenings*, which came out about ten years after Eddie's *The Wine Cellar*. And I wonder if DeMott knew if I was a great friend of Eddie's? Who knows? That might account for something because the review was such a disaster. The way it went, he said something of this order: "The first hundred pages of the book are brilliant, but then at that point it suffers a stroke from which it never recovers." Well, my God, three quarters of *Ancient Evenings*, I think it was seven hundred pages long, the six hundred that came after the first hundred was an awful lot of good stuff. [laughs]

Lee: Are there any other books in which you feel you were critically short-changed?

Mailer: You know, that's part of the given. You get a book and it doesn't matter whether the book is good or bad, it's going to get the same number of good and bad reviews within reason. In other words, a dreadful book will probably get three good reviews in ten and a very good book may get six good reviews in ten. It's just amazing how they tend to push to the middle in reviewing. Until you know that and know it in your bones, it's very hard to keep writing year after year, book after book, and get over those insane desires to kill a critic. And you have to be able to somehow adjust to that, otherwise you'll walk around tired all the time.

Lee: There's that great quote by Christopher Morley, "A critic is a gong at the railroad crossing, clanging loudly and vainly as the train goes by."

Mailer: [laughs] Oh well.

Lee: Some writers seem to define their fiction by a sense of place. Paul Bowles with Morocco, Tom McGuane, even Hemingway to a great extent, had the setting define his work. Since *Tough Guys Don't Dance* was your only novel set on Cape Cod, is it safe to say that a novel begins for you with character?

Mailer: Yeah, I think it's safe. I'm never happy with place or plot as the core of a novel. That's just that my abilities probably lie more in the direction of characters. I can write about place and I enjoy it, but it's not the predominant element. In fact, most of my books, I'd have to go through them one by one, but any book that's half decent is going to have a sense of place. You could say *The Naked and the Dead* has a sense of place even though that wasn't what it was intending to do. They all have a sense of place, but place worries me. I don't want to start with place, let place come into it.

Lee: Did you have the most fun writing *Tough Guys*?

Mailer: You know it's probably one of my favorite books, not because I think it's one of my best books, but because when you've written a lot of books you end up very much like an old woman who's had a great many children and says, "Oh the sixth was a wonderful delivery." So what happens, I was in terrible trouble with *Tough Guys* because I had a contract with Little, Brown and we'd come to an end. It was a lame duck contract and I had to deliver a book to them. Just before that I had written *Ancient Evenings* and I was profoundly tired. And so I took a year off while I was being paid by Little, Brown and then at the end of the year they said, where's the book? This was a one-year contract for the book. I realized I was going to be in debt for the rest of my life if I didn't give them a book because I would have had to earn so much to pay off what they paid me for that year. So not wanting to live like Joe Louis, playing catch-up all the time, I thought, well, I've got to write this book and I've got to write it in two months. And I thought, I might have to go into the tank. It was the first and only time I ever said that to myself—I may have to write a bad book. I'm just going to give them a book and fuck 'em. Fuck 'em. So I sat down to write it and I thought, how am I going to write a book in two months? Well, I'll tell it in the first person because that lends itself to easier writing on a daily basis. So who am I going to have as a narrator? Well, he has to be enough like me so it's comfortable, but he mustn't be exactly like me because then I'll get all wound up with myself. So I thought, all right, a writer who's much younger than me, not successful, but has some of my mentality—not completely, different. I'll make him one-quarter Jewish and half Irish and one-quarter Protestant; that'll be general enough. And then that was the one time I thought about place: Provincetown. So I started writing it and what happened was, I was prepared to write a bad book if I had to—and it's certainly not a great book or even probably a good book—but what it's got is a very good style. In fact it's one of my better-written books. I was so happy with that—that the style was good—because it's as if you're a middle-aged woman who wouldn't want to be seen without her makeup. Style is almost like makeup in that sense. So I felt that the book doesn't have to be great but if the style's good, fine. I can live with it. And the book got written in two months, the first draft, and then I had time to revise it afterwards.

Lee: It seems you've led two lives, as a novelist and a journalist with the lines occasionally blurring. Since we've been both involved in the founding of a publication called *The Voice* [Lee co-founded *The Cape*

Cod Voice; Mailer co-founded *The Village Voice*] how do you perceive journalism has evolved, if indeed you consider it an evolution?

Mailer: Oh, it's evolved, but I'm not sure I have any sharp answers on that. The level of sophistication is vastly higher, greater now, much more evident than it was in the old days. In the old days if you saw a well-written piece in a magazine, you treasured it to a degree. Now most pieces are fairly well written. That part of it is good, on the other hand there is a kind of homogeneity to magazines, even the successful ones, that I really can't bear. The prose has become the least important part of the magazines now and that's the irony—that although the prose is better, the presentation of the prose is really measly. Eight point type, nine point type, stuff like that. Colored pages flooded with ads and visuals of all sorts and the idea that someone is going to read a magazine for content is disappearing. So in that sense it's like the old human story: as things get better, so do they get worse in other ways. It's almost as the face becomes more beautiful, so do the feet rot. Most magazines by now are disappointments. I spoke to you about your magazine and I think it's the tastiest Cape Cod magazine around, for a newspaper or magazine.

Lee: That quote will definitely make it into the interview.

Mailer: [laughs] But the typography is good and you can't say that about most of the papers and magazines around. The Provincetown magazine is good—the one Chris Busa does—*Provincetown Arts*. That's good.

Lee: How do you feel about community journalism in general?

Mailer: If it's good, it's great. It changes a community, there's no question about that. It alters a community and it's a large question I don't really have a sharp answer for because I really haven't thought about it much. You know, I'm pretty much at a utilitarian level here, if there's a local newspaper or magazine that's good, I'm pleased because I live here. If they're not that good, I shrug.

Lee: What was it like being assassinated in the movie *Ragtime*?

Mailer: Oh, that's a good question. I signed on for the movie and was delighted and always wanted to work as an actor in a big mainstream movie and see what it's like. Norris and I had just gotten married and flew over to London for the film. Then it suddenly came to me, I'm going to be assassinated. What the fuck have I done? It's madness, you don't play with your life that way. You don't go through a symbolic murder of yourself. You're violating something basic and profound. And one of the things I found in life is that it's worth being a professional and my definition of a professional is you can do a decent day's work on a very bad day. So, all right, I'm a professional and I signed a contract, I agreed to do it, so I'll do it. But I was miserable. And then one or two days before I was to be assassinated, John Lennon was assassinated for real. That wiped it all out; I thought, let's stop carrying on. All your concern over this is ridiculous, this is minor, so suck it up and stop whining. When it took place, the mechanics of it were so interesting that I suffered no bad feelings while it was going on. When I was shot—and they prepare you for this by wearing a wig and under the wig they put a charge because a hole has to appear in your head with blood coming out. So there's a small explosive charge next to your scalp and as these guns go off and the blood starts spurting from me, I've got to rise from my chair and knock over a champagne bucket and then do a half gainer so I land on the floor with this tube bringing the blood up to my scalp and keeping it invisible as I land. So the athletics of that had me absolutely preoccupied and I didn't want to blow it because there are four hundred people, all the extras, watching it. I remember doing it and doing it successfully and being very pleased with myself because that's what I was concentrating on. They put wax in my ears so that the explosions wouldn't deafen me and I'd been told not to move after I hit the ground. In the meantime, Norris, who was there, had been screaming—which was called for in the role—but I couldn't even hear that. Then I feel her shaking me and I think, what's she doing? Apparently her screams were incredible and the soundman came forward, virtually with tears in his eyes and said, "That's the best sound I've heard since this movie was made." [laughs] So Norris felt very excited—oh God, I'm going to have a side occupation as a screamer. And as we're going home that day after the shoot I told her not to get her hopes up, because that scream was *too good*. I knew how well she could scream—well, no, she never screams personally, it's a professional gift as an actress. I knew they were going to hear that scream in the movie and ask who that woman was because it's just a bit part and they'll be curious and frustrated that they don't see more of her after that scream. So they're going to tone it down, which is exactly what they did. The scream was just mixed in the general brouhaha.

Lee: Did you get to talk to James Cagney much?

Mailer: No, he was almost decrepit at that point. In fact, he could hardly move. He was in his mid or late 80's at that point. He has a scene where early in the movie Harry Thaw comes in and starts attacking me as Stanford White and threatening me and talking about how he's going to expose me. And at that point, I turn in a very lordly fashion and say to him, "Why don't you address your complaints to Rheinlander Waldo [Cagney's character] who's the Chief of Police of New York?" And everyone turns to look and there's Cagney and Cagney looks back—and I was in a position to see right in his eyes—and they showed absolutely nothing. And I realized something profound about movies that I never understood before, which is he was an old vet who knew just how to do it. Because his expression was totally noncommittal, everyone who's watching all went into his eyes and everyone took out whatever interpretation they wanted. It was a perfect example of screen acting as opposed to theatrical acting and he knew it. It's a wonderful moment, but all craft of lore, nothing to do with acting.

Lee: Out of the litany of film stars, international personalities and politicians, are there any that stand out to you that you're truly glad you've met?

Mailer: Yeah, Muhammad Ali. That one's easy.

Lee: Have you seen him lately?

Mailer: I saw him four or five years ago in Indiana where he's living with his wife. Then I saw him again in New York at a party. He's still got all of his old tricks. He speaks in a very soft voice now, you can hardly hear what he says. And so he's doing what he's always able to do—he pulls you in toward him. He always had that great gift of pulling people in toward him.

Lee: I promise this is the last question.

Mailer: [laughs] You're like a camera man, Mike. Always another shot.

Lee: You once said regarding your epitaph, "He may have been a fool, but he did his best and that can't be said of all fools." Would you change that?

Mailer: Yeah, I'd change it. I'd probably go to Andre Gide's famous remark, "Please do not understand me too quickly."

James Campbell
Rectal Examination

Robert Pinsky

The Forgetting

The forgetting I notice most as I get older is really a form of
    memory:
The undergrowth of things unknown to you young, that I have
    forgotten.

Memory of so much crap, jumbled with so much that seems to matter.
Lieutenant Calley. Captain Easy. Mayling Soong. Sibby Sisti.

And all the forgettings that preceded my own: Baghdad, Egypt, Greece,
The Plains, centuries of lootings of antiquities. Obscure atrocities.

Imagine!— a big tent filled with mostly kids, yelling for poetry. In fact
It happened, I was there in New Jersey at the famous poetry show.

I used to wonder, what if the Baseball Hall of Fame overflowed
With too many thousands of greats all in time unremembered?

Hardly anybody can name all eight of their great grandparents.
Can you? Will your children's grandchildren remember your name?

You'll see, you little young jerks: your favorite music and your political
Furors, too, will need to get sorted in dusty electronic corridors.

In 1972, Zhou En-Lai was asked the lasting effects of the French
Revolution: "Too soon to tell." Remember?—or was it Mao Tse-Tung?

Poetry made of air strains to reach back to Begats and suspiring
Forward into air, grunting to beget the hungry or overfed Future.

Ezra Pound praises the Emperor who appointed a committee of scholars
To pick the best 450 Noh plays and destroy all the rest, the fascist.

The standup master Stephen Wright says he thinks he suffers from
Both amnesia and déjà vu: "I feel like I have forgotten this before."

Who remembers the arguments when jurors gave Pound the only prize
For poetry awarded by the United States Government? Until then.

I was in the big tent when the guy read his poem about how the Jews
Were warned to get out of the Twin Towers before the planes hit.

The crowd was applauding and screaming, they were happy— it isn't
That they were anti-Semitic, or anything. They just weren't listening. Or

No, they were listening, but that certain way. In it comes, you hear it,
    and that
Selfsame second you swallow it or expel it: an ecstasy of forgetting.

Gordon Weaver

That Face in My Bathroom Mirror

That is no country for old men.
W. B. Yeats, "Sailing to Byzantium"

The male's awareness that one is aging—the certitude that one *has* aged—comes in small, but cumulative increments, starkly dramatized from time to time by epiphany-like shocks. The routine of morning ablutions, for example, is interrupted, without warning, by a freeze-frame glimpse of one's visage in the bathroom mirror, mid-shave or mid-rinse, wholly unanticipated. Who is *that*? Is that *me*? Indeed it is. Face it!

Women, by custom, may and do retard or mitigate such evidence in their vanity's glass—dyes and moisturizing lotions, cosmetics and cosmetic surgeries, chemical injections. But male pride, also by custom, requires a stoic survey of the evidences of the ravages of Time.

One's hair, once a crowning glory, has evolved into a ragged, thinning cap, the hairline having crept upward and backward. Glossy auburn richness has faded to a streaky, dingy gray. Is that *me*? The custom of masculine courage demands an honest attention to detail. Face it.

How came that sallow complexion (intensified by fluorescent lighting)? When did laugh lines degenerate into indelible furrows in the brow, alongside the mouth, at the eyes' corners? The nose is decidedly more prominent, as are the ears (from which sprout clumps of bristle as snowy white as one's whiskers). Lips once seductively plump have compressed to a thin, pale line more suggestive of anger than resolve. Yellowing teeth are longer. And eyes, once bright with expectation and delight, are now muddy, purging in sleep, as Hamlet said of Polonius, rheum, one's vision reliant on the assistance of ever-thicker bifocals. And one's throat has risen, dewlap seeming intent on swallowing the chin above.

Elizabeth I, in her sixties, termed by Raleigh "a woman surprised by time," had her palace mirrors removed, of course to no avail. Just so, one shuns reflective surfaces (shop windows, polished metal or wood) and expresses reluctance to be caught in candid snapshots, averts one's glance, feeling vaguely shamed, when producing a picture ID to board an airplane or cash a check. Family albums stay on the shelf, dramatizing as they do, year by decade, all that has been lost. Or, put another way, that went away. The supermarket checkout clerk, on the other hand, asks for no identification, simply ringing up the obvious geezer's senior discount. Time.

It is easier, for shorter or even longer periods, to ignore—if not forget—the gross remainder of one's corporeal self. But honesty, an aspect of courage for either gender, compels itemization.

One's skin, over hands, arms, torso, legs, shines an almost luminescent white, speckled randomly overall with (pre-cancerous?) wens. And the backs of those hands display nascent liver spots and the irremovable tobacco tinge on the first and second digits of one's smoking hand. And to flex a bicep is to invite at worst depression or, at best, comic ridicule. Joints: the creaking, knobby knees, the puckered gathering at elbows of something akin to medium-grade sandpaper, the dull ache that flares or persists across one's lower back. Buttocks—be grateful for small mercies!—have shrunk to hollows rather than ballooned. Long legs that once carried one with some grace and some speed on the hardwood court or playing field have morphed into fragile pipestems, horny feet and gnarled toes. The body, as Richard Pryor put it (or was it Ali?), should sue these legs for non-support.

Most any exertion, no matter how slight—bending to pick a pencil off the carpet, reaching high to change a light bulb—leaning too far left or right, provokes an audible, unwilled grunt, followed by a stifled sigh of relief, and resignation. And one's height has diminished an inch, maybe two, this loss accentuated by an incipient dowager's hump. Visible in profile or full frontal, one's gut sags too low to be sucked up, what Farrell's Studs Lonigan called an *alderman*. Oh the gluttony, oh the drink!

Honesty. Consider within this too unsolid flesh.

One's breath is halt—oh the unfiltered Camels! The voice is scorched to a rasp after too many exuberant words. AM and PM hacking like a sick cat, wheezing like an asthmatic, are routine. A once cast-iron stomach, fond of hot spices, rich sauces, and every variety of meat, now grumbles and rumbles after even bland fare, sending forth an involuntary chorus of burps and belches ill-concealed behind a clenched fist. And oh the fits of farting, near-impossible to suppress in polite company! Satisfactory defecation is now a daily goal and ordeal. A bladder once capacious necessitates a bathroom stop before even short-distance travel, a ritual one remembers imposed by parents in childhood. The urgent need to urinate rouses one from sleep often enough to suggest (knock wood!) a failing prostate or (knock again) the onset of diabetes.

Do be honest! One's member is no longer consistently erect upon waking. Viagra and like supplements tempt, but the caution that erections lasting more than four hours should be reported to one's physician (as well worthy of informing the *Guiness Book of Records!*) puts paid to such notions. Still there are pills (cholesterol, blood pressure), and over-the-counter nostrums (Tums, Maalox, Alka-Seltzer, Pepto Bismol).

And as with the body, so goes the mind.

The quality of sleep has degenerated. Instead of the solid six-eight hours, slumber is broken into larger or smaller bits and pieces: micturation signals through dreams in which nature's call is loud and clear, narratives placing one in frantic search of a lavatory that never materializes, or pissing a stream accompanied by an electric buzzing and vibration; with no discernible cause, one wakes suddenly and fully, the prospect of further sleep improbable at best. Dawn's first light in the bedroom window gives notice it's over for yet another night. Utterly gone is the ability to crash hard, sleep off a late-night carouse or recover from unaccustomed physical exertion.

And one's recurring dreams are now ridden with futility and fear. Again and again, one is stricken with paralysis when flight from danger is called for. Weapons misfire, strength fails, answers to profound questions elude. Now, in place of the usual bizarre violent action or randy sex, dreams are peopled with faces and names not consciously recalled for decades: childhood friends, grammar school teachers, old army buddies, long-dead relatives come from the grave to mystify and tease and torment. And what of the frequent dreams in which one has committed unpardonable sins or crimes, the fear of exposure lingering for moments after the shock of waking, dissipating to a foolish gratitude that none of this was real?

What source, save for aging, explains the loss of restorative sleep? To sleep, as the Bard had it, perchance to dream; but the raveled sleeve of care is not knitted up.

Out and about in the quotidian world of wakefulness, one enjoys longer or shorter spans of forgetfulness, untroubled by the facts of life, the fact of aging. But as in the bathroom mirror, come moments not to be denied, unbidden, unprovoked—or so they seem.

The aged are everywhere, in the aisles and at the Piggly Wiggly checkout. They annoy, irritate. Why must that frail granny pause her cart directly in one's path? Why must that wizened gramps take so long to write a check with trembling hand? Why does that doddering ancient back up his car without looking behind him first? Does that scrawny or semi-obese septuagenarian not realize how absurd her too-red or too-black hair coloring looks? Does that shuffling codger not know his spider's legs, purple-veined, are pathetic in walking shorts? On senior-discount-day the canes, walkers, and motorized chairs abound.

In the midst of one's arrogance and intolerance, a discomforting insight floods one's consciousness: these pensioners are one's peers! How, the question strikes one, am I attired, coifed? Does my gait betray me? Is there a tremor in my digits as I pluck at bills in my wallet? Am I one of *them*? Indeed. Face it.

And though there are palliatives for the body, pills for cholesterol and blood pressure and constipation, aspirin regimen, periodic upgrades in prescription eyeglass lenses, no relief exists to ease the chaos that assaults one's mind.

Senior Moments are scary. There are times you can't recall the title of a favorite poem or the name of a former colleague. Does noun-failure signal something truly sinister just over the horizon? A list of the day's errands is worthless if one forgets to pocket it before leaving to shop, and worthless, when pocketed, if one neglects to consult it, finds it still in that pocket after returning home?

Worse is the realization that curmudgeonly scorn threatens to become a permanent mindset toward the surrounding world. Politics, local, national, international, are swamps of corruption, nests of vipers, theaters of the absurd, asylums of the insane. Culture is Big Business in a mask. What once gave joy now annoys and angers. Art is pretense and self-indulgence and exhibitionism. One's neighbors not yet past the bloom of youth are utterly uninteresting and unattractive. How came contemporary fashion and music and literature to be so superficial, so blatantly stupid, effete, and hollow? Why have civility, manners, and style disintegrated? One cannot even ogle the nubile, indulge a propensity for the fleeting pleasure of thought-lechery, without feeling shameful, a classic Dirty Old Man.

A retreat into one's past—nothing in the present suffices, a future unimaginable—fails to console. Examined from an aged man's perspective, successes now seem trivial, failures monumental. Regret is a nagging companion; what was foolishly attempted, what wrongly pursued, what wholly undone. Like Charlie Brown at bat, why didn't I swing, why did I just stand there? The past is just that: past. Children are grown, rightly and totally embedded in their own lives. One will never know grandchildren too young who live half a continent away. And there are too many already dead in the past, family, friends, the celebrated and the obscure.

Reading the daily obituaries is a fixed routine. How old? Of what cause? An acquaintance? A morbid habit one cannot seem to break.

And when one looks squarely into that bathroom mirror, what's behind that worn face? A vision, a glimpse of the dark at the end of the tunnel.

Face it.

James Campbell
Vanity in Vain

James Brown

Some Kind of Animal

My obsession for muscle comes to an abrupt and sudden end along a narrow, two-lane mountain highway. This is the dead of winter. The night before it had snowed lightly, the roads are now slick and icy, and because in years past I'd spun out and nearly wrecked my car, I know to drive carefully. I own an older BMW 325, and I'm making slow but safe progress when a Dodge Ram suddenly appears in my rearview mirror.

Initially I ignore it.

I even look for a place to turn out and let him by, but there is none. As we continue down the highway he edges closer and closer to my bumper, until his big front grill fills my entire back window. My heart begins to pound, and I ease up on the accelerator. That's when he flips on his high beams and two sets of bright fog lamps, which combined are nothing short of blinding. My face feels hot. My ears ring and then, without further warning, I snap. When he lays on his horn I pull the wheel of my BMW hard to the left, so that the car spins sideways, blocking both lanes and trapping him. Now I have the son of a bitch exactly where I want him, and I don't care how big he is. I don't care if he's a tough guy or a coward.

Jumping out of my car, I want only one thing and that is blood.

At the time of this altercation I am bench pressing 325 pounds. I am squatting close to 400, and have, according to my girlfriend, no visible neck. At 5'8 I weigh 195, nearly all of it muscle, no small achievement for a guy who only ten months earlier topped the scales at a mere 150.

It would be convenient, in terms of a psychological profile, to suggest that my obsession with muscle stems from an inferiority complex related to my short stature. But that would only be partially true, for it is a combination of factors that fuel my passion, among them middle-age. At forty-two I feel that I'm losing my edge. I'm not as energetic. I fatigue more easily and my sexual drive isn't what it used to be. To compound matters, I have, for the better part of my life, strayed as far from the path of physical and mental health as one possibly can without entirely self-destructing. That is to say I spent the majority of my years on this planet under the influence of various and sundry illicit substances, all of which extracted a heavy toll on my body and soul. When I "bottom out," as they say in Alcoholics Anonymous, Narcotics Anonymous and Cocaine Anonymous—I've earned lifetime memberships in them all—I am a pale, gaunt, middle-aged English professor with stick-like arms and a pencil-thin neck.

My goal, other than to stay sober, is to rebuild the body I've ravaged with booze and dope. At first all I want is to feel and look healthy, maybe tone my body and get my wind back. For the average Joe achieving these goals would seem more than enough. After all most men would kill just to lose their pot bellies, let alone add a couple of inches of muscle to their arms. And under normal circumstances, for the normal person, this is where it would stop. This is where you're supposed to be happy with the improvements you've made and work now only to maintain them.

But I am not a normal person.

I have what in layman terms is called an addictive personality, and what I do, basically, is transfer my addiction to booze and dope to the healthier obsession of pumping iron.

I work out like a demon, two hours a day, five days a week. I eat well. I get eight hours of sleep every night. I subscribe to *Muscle & Fitness* and *Flex* magazine. I drink foul tasting protein shakes and spend a small fortune on body building supplements whose companies make ridiculous claims and promises when in fact their products deliver very little. After six months of intense, grueling workouts I gain a measly seven pounds.

The solution, I think, is to work out even harder, and so I do. Longer hours. Heavier weights. After a couple of months with this approach I actually *lose* several pounds and every day feel drained and worn out, like I have a perpetual hangover. It's called over-training, and I later learn that it has the reverse effect on muscle, causing it to weaken rather than grow.

In the beginning I admire the guys with lean hard bodies, and I want to look like them, but as time passes I find myself more intrigued with the bigger, more muscular physiques of the hard-core body builders. I like the idea of power. I like the idea of strength. This is also around the time when I notice that these bigger guys don't work out as hard as me and yet they make more obvious gains. Where they're benching 300 or 400 pounds, I'm stuck at 200, and have been for months. No matter how hard I try, I just can't seem to break past that 200 mark, and I don't understand what I'm doing wrong. Am I over the hill at forty-two? Do I lack testosterone? Is it the curse of bad genes? I have no answers, but over the course of the next several weeks I make friends with one of these bigger guys. For reasons of privacy, I won't divulge his real name, though I will say that among the gym rats he is endearingly referred to as Oak Junior, named after his idol, Arnold Schwarzenegger, the original Oak and Governor of the Golden State.

One morning he asks me to spot him on the bench press. He has eight plates on the bar for a total weight of 405 pounds. This is a warm up.

"I'm going for eight reps," he says.

Without breaking a sweat, he knocks them off. I shake my

head in amazement. Then I ask him, point blank, how he does it. How he got so strong, so big. Oak Junior laughs. He has two words for me.

"The Juice."

"What?"

"D-Bol, man," he says. "The Big E. Deca. Winnie-V. Tes-C." He looks me up and down and smiles. "No offense, but a few years ago I was a skinny little geek just like you."

I ignore the insult.

What peaks my interest are those strange sounding names. I have no idea what they mean, but I'll find out soon enough, when Oak Junior and I take a trip to Tijuana, about a two-hour drive from my home in the mountains of Southern California. The main drag is Revolution Boulevard and it's little more than pharmacies and tourist shops offering leather vests, jackets, cheap jewelry and switchblades. I follow Oak Junior through the crowded streets, down another block, off the beaten path and into an animal supply and feed store.

"What're we doing here?" I ask.

But Oak Junior ignores me. In a place like this I'd expect to find Mexican farmers and ranchers, and there are two or three, but the others are all Americans—two teenagers, one young woman with abnormally wide shoulders, and three clean-cut burly guys. Cops, I think. In Southern California, it's rumored that many are on the juice.

The store smells of alfalfa and barnyard manure. Behind us, stacked on top of each other, are cages with parakeets, puppies, rabbits and ducks, and secured in a glass case nearby are the accoutrements of rooster fighting—the shiny chromed spikes, razors and gaffs that attach to the leg of the gamecock. And behind the counter, directly ahead of us, are shelves and shelves of little bottles and boxes. Oak Junior points to one and the clerk passes it to him.

"This is good shit," he says to me.

But it has the picture of an animal on the label. I look more closely.

"That's a *dog*," I say.

He shrugs and turns the box over. On that side it has a picture of a bull.

"Dog, bull, what's the difference? It all works the same."

The substance is straight, unadulterated testosterone. We buy that and more, and later on the ride back home I learn, for instance, that the Big E stands for Equipoise, a steroid given to race horses, as is Winnie-V, chemically known as Stanazol. And D-Bol, a long time staple of the athletic community, is equally popular in the cattle industry. All of these drugs are injected with a syringe. All of these drugs are "stacked," administered together in various dosages and combinations, making for a potent steroid cocktail.

In the days to come I learn when and where to best stick myself with the needle: it's typically done on a weekly basis, shooting directly into a muscle, the least painful area being the buttocks. Most importantly, Oak Junior schools me on the host of other drugs you need to counter the potential side-effects of steroid use. For testicle shrinkage, you take the fertility drug, Human Chorioic Gonadrotropin, or simply HCG, which is manufactured from the urine of pregnant women. To combat gynecomastia, otherwise known in body building circles as "bitch tits," you need Clomid, another fertility drug used to induce ovulation in women. For water retention, a common side effect of testosterone usage, you take the powerful diuretic Lasix, normally prescribed for edema and serious cases of high blood pressure.

In six months, armed with this knowledge, I'm benching 300 and have gained twenty-five pounds. My medium-sized shirts no longer fit. I can't get into my regular 501's anymore and have to buy relaxed-fit. As for my boxers, they go into the rag pile, too, because I can't get them around my thighs without cutting off the circulation.

My girlfriend feels compelled to enlighten me one evening. We are stretched out in bed, having just made love for the second time in the last hour or so. For sex drive certain steroids, especially injectable testosterone, are superior to the fleeting effects of the most popular ED drugs.

"Look at your legs," she says.

"What about them?"

She makes a face.

"It's like they're growing tumors."

She is referring to my *vastus lateralis*, that is to say the outer thigh muscle, which I am quite proud of having developed.

"And your shoulders, too. You better stop taking that stuff. Seriously," she says, "you're starting to look like some kind of animal."

I draw my hand along her arm. I let it slide down between her legs and she pushes me away.

"Enough is enough," she says. "Leave me alone. It isn't fun anymore."

Then she rolls out of bed and begins to dress. I reluctantly do the same, and as I'm slipping into my relaxed-fit Levis I glance at myself in the dresser mirror. The comment she'd made about me looking like some kind of animal seems far-fetched. I take pride in those tumors on my legs. I take pride in the width and girth of my shoulders and how each muscle—the anterior, medial and posterior deltoid—are clearly defined. I admire the line of my traps, how they complement my lats and form a clear triangle of muscle through the middle of my back. In the mirror, to my eyes, I see something completely different than my girlfriend: to her I'm overblown and muscle-bound, to me I look cut and solid, anything but overbuilt.

So for the next few months I continue my quest for more muscle, for that rock-solid physique, and to this end I increase the length and intensity of my workouts. I increase the dosages of steroids. And because protein is the building block for muscle, I increase my diet, too, and eat like a pig. Each morning I consume a dozen egg whites and wash them down with a quart of milk. At lunch I devour two or three chicken or tuna sandwiches and put away another quart of milk. For dinner, more often than not, I eat blood rare steaks.

I grow.

Like a bull, I think. Big. Strong.

Now I wear an extra large T-shirt. The once loose, relaxed-fit Levis are no longer loose or relaxed. Instead they are skin-tight and the inside of my thighs rub together when I walk. Clearly, at least to others, I've undergone a radical physical mutation, but less noticeably, at least to myself, I experience another, more insidious sort of metamorphosis.

With the increased energy level from the steroids, almost like a speed high, I sleep on average about four to five hours a night. Of course that sort of schedule eventually takes a toll on my moods, and I often find myself irritated by things that never used to bother me before. I'm short with friends. I'm short with colleagues, and in the classroom, when I'm teaching, I become increasingly less patient with my students. My temper is not, as they say, at a slow boil: one second I can be perfectly calm, and then, in the next, I might suddenly lose it. Once, while I'm reading the newspaper, I come across an article that upsets me, something to do with politics, and I throw the paper on the floor and begin stomping on it, jumping up and down when my girlfriend happens into the room.

"What're you doing?"

"Nothing," I say, sheepishly.

"Look at you," she says. "Your face is all red. You're sweating."

"I'm just a little upset."

"Jim," she says, "it's not normal to get that crazy over the newspaper. Don't you see what those steroids are doing to you? You're losing it. You're flipping out over nothing."

Of course, like any good alcoholic or addict, I'm well practiced in the art of denial, and I can't for the life of me understand why she's blowing this minor incident so completely out of proportion.

"Relax," I tell her. "I'm fine. I have everything under control."

·

Under normal circumstances I rarely act on my hostile impulses. I may get mad, even furious, and on occasion justifiably so, but almost always my better judgment prevails. Almost always I'm in control. Unfortunately the incident along that narrow, two-lane mountain road is not one of those occasions. Imbued with a sense of invincibility, my anger fueled by steroids, I approach the Dodge Ram and yank open the door.

Techno music blasts from inside. He's just a kid, nineteen at most. He throws his hands up in front of his face.

"Hey, take it easy," he says. "I didn't mean nothing, man."

I grab him around the throat with one hand. He has on a baseball cap turned backwards and it falls off. I look him hard in the eyes.

"Stay off my ass," I say.

The kid doesn't move, not even to try and break away, and it might've ended there, and I wish it had. But when I let him go, as I start back to my car, he opens his fool mouth.

"Fuck you," he says.

I turn around.

"What'd you say?"

"You heard me, asshole."

In a matter of seconds he's gone from being fearful to defiant, and it's a big mistake, one that costs us both. I walk back to his truck. I reach for his neck again only this time he pulls away and takes a swing at me. The blow glances off my arm and I grab him by the collar and yank him out of the truck. His shirt rips and he falls to the ground, and as he's getting to his feet I hit him good on the side of the head, square in the temple, then again in the nose. I feel the cartilage give under my fist and then there is blood. Lots of it. All down the front of his bright white T-shirt.

The fight could've gone on. I could've hurt him worse, and I wanted to, if not for this voice in my head telling me *no, stop, enough.* The last thing I remember about that kid is the look of sheer terror on his face. The rest is kind of a blur. I don't remember, for instance, walking back to my car. I don't remember driving off. It's called a "red-out," like the alcoholic "black-out," where there's a lapse in memory. But there's no forgetting what happened about five minutes later: just a few miles up the road the Highway Patrol pulls me over, and the next thing I know my hands are flat on the roof of his cruiser. He's patting me down.

"But it was self-defense," I lie.

In the reflection of the passenger window, as I try to talk my way out of this mess, I see a stranger. In the reflection I see the face of an animal, distorted with rage and bloated from the steroids, and I hear my girlfriend's voice. I hear it, finally, loud and clear. Ahead the road glistens with rain, the asphalt black and shiny, melting away the dangerous ice.

Billy Collins

Song of the Balding

While losing mine
I have endured decades of hair

first greased
into a perfect wave about to break

then long and straight
shaken over a set of drums

then blowdried,
sitting up there like a cake.

Damn them all.
I look forward to my dome,

my resemblance to St. Paul's
and the genius of Christopher Wren.

James Campbell

Balding

photo by Minna Proctor

Thomas E. Kennedy

I Am Joe's Prostate

The year is 1994. You are 50 years old. It is three domiciles and one wife ago. In the bathroom of your somewhat classy north Copenhagen bungalow, you stand over the porcelain and pee. You have not yet learned the word *micturate*. You are so innocent. Finished, you wash your hands and open the door, startled to find your wife of twenty years' marriage listening there.

She says, "You piss like an old man." She is a physician. She says, "You need to have that checked. I'll make an appointment for you."

Three weeks later, you ride your classic, green, three-speed Raleigh twenty-five minutes north to G_____ Hospital. Through the maze of hallways without a thread or a clue as to what you are about to experience, you find the urology department. An extremely large Senior Resident with no nameplate on the pocket of his white coat extends his extremely large hand of extremely large fingers and mumbles his name. His first name. Surnames here, you will learn, are not offered, delivered only begrudgingly upon explicit request.

With a file under his arm, Dr. Mumble leads you into an examination room, has you remove your pants and perch on your knees on a metal, paper-decked table. Without prelude or warning, he rams a long fat finger up your kazoo.

You bellow, then croak, "Is that supposed to hurt so much."

"It varies," he says absently, his back to you, washing his

fingers at a sink, and continues, "There is a certain enlargement, but not more than might be expected for your age." You wonder what it is that has a certain enlargement. You finally, some years ago, learned about the existence of the clitoris, but still know nothing of the prostate. Dr. Mumble looks in the file — *your* file, instructs you to go to the nurses' station for further instructions. There you are given a large glass of colored water to drink and directed by a woman in white into a long narrow room where you are further instructed to micturate into an odd-looking steel vase with a slanted, recessed lid. Kindly, the woman in white steps out and shuts the door. You understand intuitively what micturate means, recognize it as the word of choice here in the land of white and yellow.

The odd-looking steel vase, however, does not look like something you would *want* to micturate in. Nonetheless, you do so. The slanted recessed lid flutters like a butterfly under your stream, causing a kind of needle on a machine you only just noticed to zigzag along a moving belt of graph paper. When the last few drops have dripped, causing the needle to twitch and fall still, you zip away that of you which most rarely sees the light of day and wonder what to do. You have no further instructions. Perhaps you should just go home. Yes, perhaps that is what you should do.

But the woman in white is waiting outside the door for you. You notice that she has beautiful eyes and very sensuous lips. You caution yourself not to occupy your imagination with such details in your current situation, and the woman in white with sensuous lips turns you over to another of her sort, though larger of build and darker of complexion. She leads you into another room and instructs you to undress. You have never been naked in front of a strange woman unless the object was hanky-panky.

Everything? you wonder, but trust she will say stop at the appropriate moment.

"You can leave your shirt on," she says with a smile, and you think of Joe Cocker and wonder if she is teasing you. There is no nametag at her breast pocket, and she has mumbled neither her name nor her rank. She pats an examination table, indicating that you are to lie there. Face up, you presume. You do as you are told, noting distantly how passive you have become.

She takes your penis in her fingers. *Your penis!* She sprays something into it. You say, "*Ow!*"

"Yes," she whispers and begins to stuff some manner of wire down your penis. You are rather amazed that such things go on so close to the civilized streets on which you until today so innocently dwelt. It reminds you of a scene in an Alfred Hitchcock film. *Frenzy.* It occurs to you that some men would no doubt pay a great deal of money to have a woman perform this kind of act and curse your imagination, turn your eyes away from her lips which are also rather sensual. You concentrate on not noticing the sensation of her fingers touching you, but anyway there seems no real danger that the jaunty head of Eros will poke up here.

She says, "Tell me when you feel the urge to micturate."

You felt the urge to micturate the instant she started stuffing that wire into you. Now you notice that the remainder of the wire is attached to another machine, the nature or function of which you are not destined to come to know.

You say, "Now, please."

She encourages you to stand before another metal vase and says, "You may micturate now."

Nothing happens.

She taps her foot.

Nothing happens.

She says, "Would you like me to wait outside?"

"Yes, please."

She withdraws. Still nothing happens.

When she returns she looks into the empty vase and sighs. "It would seem you didn't really have to micturate," she says.

"I thought I did."

She hums. "Well, we'll just have to try again."

It seems to you this would be an appropriate moment for her to stroke your hair and say, "You poor guy, you, it will all be over shortly, I promise," but instead she says, "Back on the table."

Having finally successfully micturated to her satisfaction, you anticipate release back into the world of clothing where private parts are truly private. Indeed, you are allowed to dress, but are then led into yet another room, instructed to lie on yet another table and left alone for a bit, perhaps to examine your conscience and feel guilty about the fact that you didn't really have to micturate before, but only said so to make her stop shoving that wire in. At length, two women come in, and you are instructed to open your pants. Why does this not surprise you? And why are you not surprised not to know their names or professions? You might ask, but there have been so many nameless people by now that it hardly seems to matter.

The taller, dark-haired of the two women seems to be in charge. She tugs your pants down to your pubis, applies some oil and lays a flat round metal thing the size of a small saucer on your pubic hair. She slides it around a bit. You notice she is looking not at you but at a screen alongside.

"Excellent," she says. "Your bladder is completely empty. Nothing is left. Excellent."

You ask, "May I go home now then, please?"

"Won't be long," she says. "Please wait here."

Presently another woman in white enters. "You'll have to take off all your clothes except your shirt," she says.

You wonder about your socks, but think, *Fuck it!* Back on the table, naked but for your unbuttoned shirt, and suddenly half a dozen people, men and women, tramp in and surround the table you are on. No one is identified, but a familiar face appears amidst them—that of the very large Senior Resident with very large fingers. All things considered, you are glad that you are lying on your back. To put you at ease, he peers down into your face with a terrifying smile and says, "I bet this won't be nearly as bad as you fear."

Then he is inserting a wand the thickness of three or four pencils into Private Johnson while he and the other unidentified people peer alternately at you, at a screen, at you, at a screen.

The wand seems to have been plunged into the very pit of your soul where it is being stirred around. You groan, but it elicits no attention or relief. You cross your arms and groan louder. Someone, a woman, tries to uncross your arms to pin your hands down which seems to you a very odd thing for her to want to do. You decide to make a stand. Your arms are crossed and will stay that way, and you set free all the groans within you, listening with some obtuse comfort to their melody, flooding from your chest in minor key.

The very large Senior Resident peers into your face unsympathetically and snaps, "Would you please *stop that!*"

But you and your groans are working together now, at last you have a partner and you will not let him go until that wand is removed from your inner sanctum.

When the thing is out, you lie groggily on the table. A woman in white hands you a pail. "You may have to micturate," she says.

How can I micturate when my bladder has just been pronounced excellently empty? you wonder, but micturate you do. It comes in pints and quarts. You note the level of micturition rising toward the lip of the pail and croak, "Nurse! Another bucket, *hurry*, please!"

At last, dressed again, dazed, you sit in a chair alongside a desk in an empty room, waiting. You do not know what you are waiting for. No doubt you have been told to wait. Thoughts of escape no longer find refuge in your consciousness. You wait. The door opens. The large Senior Resident appears with the same thin folder under his arm. *Your* folder.

He smiles at you. "Did you have a bad time of it?" he asks.

"It was no picnic lunch in the Tivoli Gardens," you say, but your bravado rings lame even in your own ears.

He sits, opens the file. "Okay," he says. "We can offer two forms of treatment. Surgical or pharmaceutical."

You don't even think to ask treatment for what. Instantly, you yelp, "Pharmaceutical, please." *No incisions.*

"Don't dismiss the surgical possibility," he says earnestly. "It is by far the fastest and most effective." He looks at you expectantly.

"I think I should prefer the pharmaceutical," you say.

"*Pre-cision*," he says, making a ring of finger and thumb and jolting it. "With surgical precision we can take the thinnest slice or two, thin as the thinnest salami slices, thinner. I urge you to consider it. It's safe and precise. I'm required to tell you about the possibility of side effects but the chances are *extremely* slight."

"Of...?"

"Uh, impotence. And incontinence. I am required to tell you that. But it is highly unlikely. Unlikely. With this procedure you won't have to be getting up two or three times in the middle of the night to urinate any more."

You say, "I don't get up in the middle of the night to urinate. Only like if I drink a bottle of beer at bedtime."

He furrows his brow, looks at the folder on his desk. "Here it says that you do."

"Well," you hear yourself say, "I am sitting right here and telling you that I don't. So what it says there is not correct."

The very large Senior Resident juts out his lower lip. He looks very sad. For reasons unknown, you thank him as you slip out the door.

The thirty minute bicycle ride to your office is not the most pleasant you have ever experienced. Each of the morning's invasions is echoed in every bump and pothole and curbstone that the rims of your Raleigh strike. At the office, your wife phones to ask how things went.

"Everything's fine," you say. "There was nothing wrong with me."

Epilogue

A dozen years, two domiciles, one wife, and no medical problems later, a routine blood test teaches you a new scrap of scientific terminology: PSA. The letters stand for Prostate Specific Antigen, but that sounds even more cruelly clinical than the simple, jaunty 'PSA.' You learn that PSA should not be higher than 4, but yours is 6.9. A follow-up sample shows it to be 12. By now you know what that very large Senior Resident was talking about slicing like a salami—your prostate. You might have known this sooner if only the *Reader's Digest* had included an article entitled "I am Joe's Prostate" in their talking organ series back in the '50s. But you know now how good your little walnut-sized prostate has been to you all these years, with what joy it has assisted.

Although you have no symptoms—no prostate enlargement, no urinary difficulties, no pain—the elevated PSA alarms your GP sufficiently to send you once again for tests—this time to F_____ Hospital. Here the personnel seem considerably more like human beings than they did at G_____ Hospital. They have names and identify themselves as doctors or nurses, and this time you are equipped with questions and a pad and pen. You write everything down. You are alert to the possibility that they may endeavor to insert foreign objects into narrow hypersensitive places, and you are determined not to allow them to do so. So determined are you that they measure your blood pressure at 160 over 120. But this time, they navigate another canal, through the backdoor with ultrasound needles. You are told that there will be some discomfort but no real pain.

There is terrific discomfort and real pain as well. Each time the doctor positions the needle and aims, watching the ultrasound screen, he says by way of warning, "And...*now!*" and something painfully uncomfortable happens somewhere you have never felt anything but pleasure before. You engage in a philosophical discourse with yourself as to the differentiation between discomfort and pain.

First, they take six biopsies. No cancer. Then they take thirteen more biopsies. No cancer. But your PSA has now risen to 15. They take twelve more biopsies. By now, after 31 biopsies, you are urinating and ejaculating blood, but still no cancer is found. Your PSA drops to 9, hops back to 12, up to 19, back down to 14, up to 18, down to 13, up to 20. Once your prostate has recovered from all the probing and sticking, you have no further signs of blood in your urine or seed.

But there is a tall, slender long-faced chief physician there at F_____ Hospital who knows, who *intuits*, that the cancer is there. He reminds you of the policeman Porfiry Petrovitch in *Crime & Punishment*. Or a taller, morose version of Lt. Columbo of the LAPD. They have not yet found it but it is there he assures you. He is, in fact, eighty percent sure it is there and fifteen percent sure that it has already spread. But he can do nothing until he has the hard evidence: a cancer cell. He wants to take a scrape of your prostate. He wants to put you into full narcosis (that's where they stop your heart and lungs for a while and keep you alive by the grace of a machine) and scrape the tiny five percent portion of your prostate where the ultrasound needles can't reach. Then you will come out of narcosis, and he will send the tissue sample to the pathologists for determination of whether there are malignant cells present.

Your ex-wife was a pathologist. She once revealed to you how difficult it is to determine malignancy. Sometimes healthy cells are falsely identified as malignant. Sometimes malignant cells are falsely identified as healthy. She quit practicing because the hospital administration was pressuring her to make too many fast decisions about what was and was not malignant.

This long-faced morose physician who is convinced that cancer is present in your prostate, which has otherwise been so good to you for half a century, will then, once he has found the cancer, be able to make a diagnosis and offer treatment. The treatment he urges will be removal of the prostate. All of it.

"You're fortunate," he tells you. "You're still young, and the cancer is very early. You can be completely cured."

Of the cancer that might not be there. Any possible side effects?

"There is a risk, I am obliged to tell you, that the scrape could result in impotence and/or incontinence."

And removal of the prostate?

"That will lead to impotence and incontinence. But the worst likely side-effect of the scrape, which is not very likely to occur at all, although I am obliged to inform you of the slight possibility, would be a modest urinary leakage and a possible reversal of your ejaculatory trajectory."

You stare at his long, morose face, his protruding eyes, and you are aware that your own face radiates the meaning of the word *aghast*. "*What, exactly*," you whisper, "does that mean?"

"Well, when you have sex, which you could continue to have quite satisfactorily by the way, you might be likely to ejaculate into your bladder instead of, well…outward. But the pleasure would be precisely the same, the sensation."

Incredulously, you tell him, "The pleasure would not be the same at all. The whole point of ejaculating is to do it into someone else! You think I'd be happy fucking my own bladder!" For one disoriented moment, you picture *impregnating* your own bladder.

"No need to be facetious," he quietly advises you. "Besides this is all quite hypothetical." His expression clearly is one he learned in a patient-management course: Deactivating the Prostate-Protection Reflex in the Recalcitrant Aging Male Patient.

You are invited into another room to watch a video entitled, *Grand Dad's Prostate Cancer*. In it, a man who has had his prostate removed plays with his two very cute grandchildren, a boy and a girl, twins of about four. He sports a wispy gray beard and has very tiny teeth; he looks into the camera and smiles a rather silly smile with his tiny white teeth. "My grandchildren think it is very funny that they have just *stopped* wearing diapers and Grand Dad has to *start* wearing them again." He chuckles.

You are not amused. You definitely do not want to wear diapers. And not that you're such a stud or anything, but you do greatly enjoy waking each morning with some lead in your pencil as indeed you cherish the occasional two-backed beast with your beloved or even the good old honeymoon of the hand. You definitely do not wish to take a permanent vacation to the land where even Viagra offers no hope. You will never willingly ejaculate into your own bladder—which seems to you of a magnitude of strangeness equal to the man in the Ripley's *Believe It Or Not*, Volume 2, Sexual Abberations, who inserted a 75 watt light bulb into his own rectum.

You develop your own future plan of treatment. You will return to the lake. On the east side of Copenhagen there is a lake you love. You love this lake because it is a street lake, in the midst of the bustling city. You have loved this lake from the moment you first spied it, thirty-four years ago. It is called Black Dam Lake, and there is an old Copenhagen proverb: *I'll go out to Black Dam Lake.*

If and when it should become necessary, on a fair and sunny day, you will rent a rowboat from the rental wharf on Black Dam Lake. You will paddle out to the center of the lake, and there you will drop anchor. You will unpack the picnic lunch you will have brought with you in a wicker basket. You will dine on smoked eel and dark rye bread spread with raw fat. Lots of it. And because fish must swim, you will drink cold bottles of beer. Many of them. And iced schnapps in your favorite Holmgaard aquavit glass, many of them. While you dine, you will watch the swans float past like beautiful white question marks. You will watch the ducks and glebes paddle along the surface, and to encourage the seagulls—for they are an important part of your plan—you will fling bits of bread and eel up into the air to get them hovering overhead in an excited, crying cluster.

And then, when you are sufficiently satisfied, sufficiently besotted but not yet incapacitated, you will take the pistol from your belt, place the barrel in your mouth, pointed upwards toward your cranial cavity and pull the trigger. It will be a high caliber pistol and will tear a broad path through your brain, spraying bits and clumps of gray matter upward, which the seagulls will catch in their beaks and gobble down, wheeling over the lake, their gullets full of morsels of your thought and personality so that you will sweep across the lake like a great pointillist consciousness on your way to forever.

Where will you get a pistol?

Oh, you'll get one. By Charlton Heston's eyes, you will!

And how can you be sure you'll be strong and deliberate enough to carry all this through when that day comes.

Well, isn't it pretty to think you might?

Coda

Nonetheless, once again, you sit in a chair before the desk of Porfiry Petrovitch.

"You must choose now," he says. "The number is very high. The disease is present. It may already have spread. I *know* this."

His protruding eyes make you think of the face in an ancient icon.

You say, "Well, I had a second opinion from ..."

"I *know* the source of your second opinion," says Porfiry Petrovitch, "both professionally and socially. He is a nice fellow and a good internist, but he is *not* a urological surgeon, and he knows *nothing* of this."

Porfiry Petrovitch is younger than you, but his eyes are stronger, his protruding eyes. You turn your own gaze from them, look out the window behind him at the slate gray sky, toward the door, which is shut and unpromising. His protruding eyes never waver from your face. They contain the words that he has spoken, that he need not repeat: "You must choose now." But he has already chosen.

So you nod. The procedure is scheduled. For three weeks you watch its inexorable approach. Then, finally, in the ward, you are dressed in a flimsy gown, being measured for support stockings, checked over like an old car, stuck with needles, thermometers, fed a pill and told it is best you get into bed because you might get woozy.

You note that you feel pretty good. Feisty even. Planning some havoc as a silent orderly rolls your bed out into the hall, the elevator up to the OR where the anesthesiologist looks soberly into your eyes and says, "We have to ask your name, standard procedure."

"My name," you say, "is Porfiry Petrovitch," giving the name of the head of the urology unit. The surgeon, alongside, laughs. "Then we'll cut right in!"

A nurse adjusts the valve set into the vein on back of your hand and the anesthesiologist does something to it, and now you are feeling very good. You cannot believe it is possible to feel this good.

"Think about something nice now," the anesthesiologist says.

You say, "I feel pretty damn good," and he whispers at your ear, "Men pay lots of money to feel the way you're feeling right now."

You do not reply. You are completely absorbed thinking about your wife, about how she looked in her aquamarine two-piece swim suit last summer on the beach at Skorpios, the surf frothing around her beautiful legs, blond, tan, smiling. She is smiling for you with her blue blue eyes, drawing you forward into her gaze, her gorgeous body…

Suddenly they're rolling you out again.

"Say, where are you taking me?" Your voice sounds slurry.

"It's over," says a nurse. "We want you down in the wake-up room for a while where we can keep an eye on you."

You open your mouth and hear yourself say, "Dr. No. Ursula Andress." This seems hilarious to you, but no one even smiles. Can they even hear you? Are you dead? Is this death? You want to explain your words but you notice a fly on the sheet, just sitting there, so still.

A while later you notice that you are hooked up to some contraption on which hangs a clear plastic bag of blood. From the bag runs a tube which disappears under your sheet. You become aware of a very annoying discomfort in the worst of places. The blood, you understand then, is your own micturition. You have been fitted with a catheter. You are given permission to get out of bed. You do so carefully, supporting yourself on the contraption from which your bag of blood hangs and to which you are connected by a long flexible tube. The contraption looks like some kind of garment rack, and you discover that it is on wheels.

For want of anything better to do, you shuffle out of the room and along the ward corridor, rolling the rattling contraption alongside you, your bag of blood swaying there. You do not like looking at the bag of blood, but it seems wherever you send your eyes, they always wander back to it, recoiling from it again, wandering back. You shuffle the length of the hall, learn how to turn your contraption without causing the connecting tube to tug at your exhausted tugger where you least want to be tugged just now. It occurs to you that all the nurses here are very good-looking, and you advise yourself not to even think about that for a second lest your tugger begin to get untoward ideas.

You begin to shuffle again, back along the corridor. Three men sit around a table, their contraptions parked alongside them as they play cards with a greasy-looking deck. "How come you don't sit down?" one of them asks as you shuffle past.

"Hurts less when I'm on my feet."

"Hurts less when he's on his feet," another man explains to the first as you proceed to shuffle the night away.

Next morning the surgeon comes in to visit. Not Porfiry Petrovitch but the smiling good-humored fellow who actually did the cutting. "Just to let you know," he says brightly, "that I took three good slices and everything looked fine. No enlargement, no irregularity. It is a good-looking prostate I saw."

"Should be," you say. "It's Joe's prostate."

They laugh as though they understand.

The surgeon returns that afternoon, a nurse alongside him, a dark-haired nurse who fills her translucent white uniform so perfectly that you have to avert your eyes for fear of losing your catheter.

"Is there still blood in his urine?" the surgeon asks her.

"The color of rosé wine," she replies.

You thank her for ensuring that you will never again for the remainder of your life drink rosé wine.

"We don't drink rosé wine here either," she says with a twinkle of regret.

"How do you feel about going home now?" the smiling surgeon asks.

Then you are alone with the nurse. You are in bed. She is alongside. She reaches under the covers. Could this be love? you wonder as she whispers, "Take a deep breath now. I'm going to remove the catheter. I'm afraid I'll have to move back your foreskin first."

"If you try to do that," you say, "we'll be here forever because I don't have one."

"Then take a breath."

You do, and you hear a strangling gargling horror-comic groan contract your throat: <u>Argh!</u> You consider that the first person who ever thought to write that sound with just those letters had been through this very procedure.

She holds it up for you to see—a thick pencil-like device with a ragged bulb on the end. She points at the bloody bulb. "That's the thing that hurts coming out."

You have just reached an understanding of what the ugliest word in the language is: *Catheter*. Three syllables of misery. Even worse in Danish: *Kateter.*

It will be a fortnight before you have the biopsy results. That, you know, is when the treatment can begin. The aim of this exercise has been to tenderize you for the real cut.

Two weeks ensue with frequent, fiery micturitions. You live in dread of the micturition urge. You have twisted the water pipe alongside your jakes into a pretzel and ground a millimeter off your molars. You sustain yourself by contemplating your hatred of the word 'catheter.' You check its etymology, hoping that it is named for its inventor so that you can put a face on your hatred, but find it is built of Greek and Latin word parts that mean something like "passing through." Every time you grit your teeth and micturate fire you consider the fact that this ugly collection of letters—some of your favorite letters of the alphabet, too, though here organized in the ugliest possible fashion—represents a device which threatens to become a long-term fixture in your life.

There will be catheters, there will be catheters… In the room the nurses come and go talking of catheters… We have lingered by the catheters of the sea by sea girls wreathed in plastic tubing… I should have been a pair of ragged catheters scuttling across the floors of rosé-colored seas.

On the appointed day, you enter the appointed consultation room and shake the hand of the smiling surgeon as well as the hand of the dark-haired nurse at his side. The dark-haired lady. There is always a dark-haired lady. Saying, "Take a deep breath now…"

You are motioned to a chair. The smiling surgeon sits, lays the flat of his palm on a folder before him on the desktop. "Well," he says, and smiles. "Nothing. There is nothing."

"Nothing?"

"No cancer. Not even a single cell. I took samples from every corner where the ultra sound needles can't reach. And there is nothing. You have a healthy prostate."

"What happened?"

"Sometimes the PSA is wrong," he says. The dark-haired nurse nods, smiles reassuringly. "Sometimes the PSA is wrong," she echoes.

Thus, after two years, twenty blood tests, thirty-four biopsies, the last three of which were surgical, and two weeks of micturating fire, you are sent out into the world, onto the sunny pavement to find your way in a world of health.

What is a man to do? Down the street and on the other side, you see a sign that says BAR. You head for it.

photo by Jean-Luc Bertini

Steve Davenport

Inside Sports

Coffee Joe's a corkball bat in a cage
outside a south St. Louis bar. Coffee Joe's
the slick white ball stitched red, two parts bullet,
one part skittery target. It's league night,
55-and-over. Meatballs are good,
the beer's ice cold, and Coffee Joe's an ass

still slick from a specialist's rubber glove.
His walnut a coconut, Coffee Joe's
a needle in his dick or an implant
and the pump under his balls. Coffee Joe

is X-marks-the-spot.

Stephen Dunn

Turning Fifty

I saw the baby possum stray too far
and the alert red fox claim it
on a dead run while the mother watched,
dumb, and, oddly, still cute.
I saw this from my window
overlooking the lawn surrounded
by trees. It was one more thing
I couldn't do anything about,
though, truly, I didn't feel very much.
Had my wife been with me,
I might have said, "the poor possum,"
or just as easily,
"the amazing fox." In fact,
I had no opinion about what I'd seen,
I just felt something dull
like a small door being shut,
a door to someone else's house.

That night, switching stations, I stopped
because a nurse had a beautiful smile
while she spoke about triage and death.
She was trying to tell us
what a day was like in Vietnam.

She talked about holding
a soldier's one remaining hand,
and doctors and nurses hugging
outside the operating room.
And then a story of a nineteen-year-old,
almost dead, whispering, "Come closer,
I just want to smell your hair."

When my wife came home late, tired,
I tried to tell her
about the possum and the fox,
and then about the young man
who wanted one last chaste sense
of a woman. But she was interested
in the mother possum,
what did it do, and if I did anything.
Then she wanted a drink, some music.
What could be more normal?
Yet I kept talking about it
as if I had something to say—
the dying boy
wanting the nurse to come closer,
and the nurse's smile as she spoke,
its pretty hint of pain,
the other expressions it concealed.

Stephen Dunn

Sixty

Because in my family the heart goes first
and hardly anybody makes it out of his fifties,
I think I'll stay up late with a few bandits
of my choice and resist good advice.
I'll invent a secret scroll lost by Egyptians
and reveal its contents: the directions
to your house, recipes for forgiveness.
History says my ventricles are stone alleys,
my heart itself a city with a terrorist
holed up in the mayor's office.
I'm in the mood to punctuate
only with that maker of promises, the colon:
next, next, next, it says, God bless it.
As Garcia Lorca may have written: some people
forget to live as if a great arsenic lobster
could fall on their heads at any moment.
My sixtieth birthday is tomorrow.
Come, play poker with me,
I want to be taken to the cleaners.
I've had it with all stingy-hearted sons of bitches.
A heart is to be spent. As for me, I'll share
my mulcher with anyone who needs to mulch.
It's time to give up the search for the invisible.

On the best of days there's little more
than the faintest intimations. The millennium,
my dear, is sure to disappoint us.
I think I'll keep on describing things
to ensure that they really happened.

Steve Heller

Pursuing Mediocrity

No matter how many vitamins I take, nor abdominal crunches I attempt, there's just no escaping the fact that my wife Sheyene (pronounced like the town in Wyoming) is nearly three decades younger than I. During our first four years together, we lived in quiet, conservative Manhattan, Kansas (the Little Apple), where just going to McDonald's could be disconcerting.

"Would your father like fries with that?"

"He's not my father."

"Excuse me, Ma'am. Would your grandfather like French fries?"

Now we live in L.A., where the difference in our ages is so unremarkable no one ever remarks on it. "You two make a cute couple," we might hear from a friend, a colleague, or a homeless person, but that's about it. Nevertheless, one ghost that continues to haunt me out here is the specter of Sheyene's lost youth. Although we have many friends her age, from time to time Sheyene tells me: "I almost never get to be young." She's right. She seldom gets to do the dumb, fun things people do when they're young.

Unless, of course, I do them with her.

Perhaps that's why we decided to move into an apartment on the Venice Boardwalk, where dumb, fun things are an established way of life. Biking, begging, juggling, hula-hooping, tattooing.

And, of course, rollerblading.

Despite our deliberate choice to live on a street where youth is regarded as a lifelong entitlement, Sheyene, who has skated since she was four, is stunned when she casually asks me one day if I'd like to learn how to rollerblade.

"Sure."

"You don't mean that."

"Yes, I do. You'll have to teach me, though."

"Oh, it's easy. It's like riding a bicycle; you never forget."

"I never rode that kind of bicycle."

It's true. Although my reply to her question was swift, the answer has been a long time coming. Even though I run and bike regularly, during my first fifty-three years neither wheels nor blades have ever adorned my definitely un-winged feet. No rollerblades, roller skates, nor ice skates. Nothing that could prepare me for what lies ahead on the Boardwalk: the specter of Steve crashing.

When Sheyene finally grasps this fact, she begins to worry. "You'll have to wear a helmet at all times—and pads for your hands, elbows, and knees."

"You don't wear anything but the hands."

Sheyene gives me a look I haven't seen since my mother caught me drawing rocket ships on her bedroom mirror with her mauve lipstick.

"OK, where do we get them?" I reply, thinking: This can't be as hard as dancing.

Sheyene already has rollerblades and hand pads. Instead of buying gear for me, we decide to rent a set first. "You know," she says, "just in case . . ."

"I kill myself on the first run?"

"Exactly. You *are* going to be careful, aren't you?"

"Of course."

Half an hour later I'm dressed like a Three Stooges astronaut as I inch my way along a blue brick wall on the side of Venice Bike & Skates, on the corner of Washington and Speedway. We've already decided that both the Boardwalk and the one-way, alley-like roadbed of Speedway contain too many obstacles and potential victims. So Sheyene pushes me along the wall like a mannequin on a flatbed dolly until we come to the even narrower alley behind Venice Bike & Skates. No bikes, no automobiles, no foot traffic.

Perfect.

"Don't forget to bend your knees and lean slightly forward," Sheyene cautions. "Even though you're wearing a helmet, you don't want to fall backwards."

"Yes, Sergeant."

"I'll be right beside you. You wanna hold my hand?"

"This isn't a damn Beatles song. Just gimme a little room."

"It's your funeral," she replies, and removes her hand from the small of my back.

I crouch on my blades like a poodle taking a crap, then let go of the wall.

"Hey, this isn't so—"

BAM!

"Oh, sweetie . . . are you OK?"

"Yeah, I'm all right." Above me, a startled pigeon flaps from one rooftop to the next. The sky is the color of blue peppermint Listerine. "I guess the helmet was a good idea . . . my legs just shot out from under me."

"I *told* you to bend your knees."

"If I bent my knees any more, I'd be sitting down." I prop myself up on my elbows so that I actually am sitting on the asphalt. When I turn my head to the left, I find Sheyene standing over me in her white shorts and pink tank top, balanced perfectly on her own wheels like a veteran car hop.

"I'd like a Sonic Burger with cheese."

"Stay right there," she replies, and skates over to a nearby dumpster. "I'm going to take off my blades so I can walk beside you and help you keep your balance."

"You don't need to take off your skates," I object, and push myself up on my palms, squatting on the pavement with my blades beneath me again. "We both know I'm going to have to fall in order to learn. So just keep your distance and watch me—"

BAM!

"Well, at least you didn't have to fall as far that time."

More the color of faded blue jeans, I decide, staring straight up again. When I roll my helmet to the left, I find Sheyene balancing herself on a single set of wheels. She's holding onto the dumpster with one hand and unlocking the skate boot on her left foot with the other.

"Oh, all right," I concede, climbing to my knees this time. I put my right hand on the wall and my left on the pavement, then slide one set of wheels beneath me, testing my balance before I try the other. "Look, damn it. I know I'm never going to be good at this, but I swear I can be mediocre."

"I'm certain you can," Sheyene says, stripping off the first boot.

Still bracing myself with both hands, I edge the second set of wheels beneath me.

"Sweetie, wait! Don't—"

Flump . . . BAM!

I raise my chin to see Sheyene hopping across the alley toward me on her bare foot. This time I'm on my belly.

"Well, that's progress," she says.

This goes on for perhaps another twenty minutes. Eventually, by taking baby steps, never letting my wheels move at all, with Sheyene's help I manage to progress forward a total of about five feet. About six inches per fall, I estimate. "You're doing *great*, sweetie," Sheyene says several times.

When we finally return the rented gear—now dented, gnarled, and scuffed like a dog's chew toy—Sheyene is shocked when I insist on purchasing a helmet, blades, and a complete set of pads right then.

"So, you're committed," the clerk says, grinning at me.

"Like Death," I reply.

And so, to Sheyene's terrified amusement, over the weeks that follow I keep at it. In the beginning I merely edge along the brown wall of the Ellison on Speedway, keeping at least one hand on the brick. Sheyene walks patiently beside me as I *BAM!* pick my way along the wall *CRACK!* like a dizzy four-legged insect trying to climb out of a bathtub *bumble-bumble-plop*. When I finally gain enough confidence to remove my hand from the wall, the results *BAM!* are similar.

But I persist. One morning a week or so later, I get up at 5:30 a.m., but do not wake Sheyene. While she sleeps, I hurry down the Boardwalk, flapping along in my rubber sandals, to the small parking lot at the end of Navy, between the Safran Senior Living Community and the Jewish Social Center. I sit down on the pavement next to the Marc Chagall mural and kick off my sandals, then strap on my blades, helmet, and pads. I shiver to my feet like a baby bird, then freeze to gain my balance. For a few seconds I just stand there motionless, a full-body sculpture mocking Chagall. Finally, with only a single yelp of fear, I push myself away from the wall—and begin to skate.

Alone.

When Sheyene finds me about half an hour later, I am still upright—and have been for a good fifteen minutes. Elated, I wave a fist in the air as I execute a shuddering turn and skate confidently back toward her. "Hey, whaddayah think?" I brag. "Not bad for an old—"

BAM!

Sheyene smiles down at me. "You're doing great, honey."

"Well, I *was*, damn it."

On the Boardwalk, a homeless guy pushing a grocery cart filled with wadded clothing and over-stuffed plastic garbage bags gives me a thumbs-up.

Like a dazed bronco rider bucked off his steed, I stagger to my wheels, slap my thighs, and shove off again.

To Sheyene's surprise and my own, I manage to skate upright for perhaps two minutes, until she finally assures me she truly is impressed. "Really, Steve. You're coming along." I can tell she's sincere, but I also know that what really gets her is the simple fact that after so many crashes I am still doing this. For her.

When at last I'm finished showing off, we discover someone has stolen my sandals.

Weeks go by. Each morning before work, I am out there, startling dog walkers and garbage collectors like Frankenstein's monster tumbling out of a tree. After a while, we decide I'm ready for the Boardwalk—in the early morning when fewer pedestrians are at risk. This strategy proves wise.

BAM!

"No harm, no foul, sweetie. You can do it."

A few days later, after I've reached a certain level of incompetence, Sheyene advances me to the bike path, even though it curves.

"Lean a little bit when you try to turn . . . That's right."

CRACK!

"Well, not exactly like that."

Finally one weekend she decides to let me loose on the Boardwalk in the afternoon, amidst the crowds. Everything goes great, until a man in a Sex Pistols T-shirt decides to stop and get a hot dog.

Thud-BAM!

"When you get up this time, sweetie, don't try to go around the tourists; let them go around you."

"Damn the casualties! Full speed ahead!" I cry, and go at it again.

The bike path is the greater challenge. In addition to a few novices like me, on any afternoon the bike path is filled with accomplished skaters of every age, leaping and spinning, slicing and dicing their way through the crowd like Speed Racers. I ignore them all and try to stay upright to avoid the domino effect:

BAMCRACKPOWTHUDWhatthehellareyouDOINGman?

But time is on my side. Each successive afternoon I fall a little less often and frighten fewer unwary civilians. The ones who recognize me move aside. No matter what, I keep going. Eventually I am able to maintain the pace of an elderly stroke victim plodding along behind a walker. Toddlers hustle past me on the adjacent grass; I smile and wave at their nervous mothers. I skate on with no regard for my health or reputation. I am relentless. I am the skinny old soldier with the battle-scarred red helmet. I am Slow-Motion Crash Dummy. I am Old Fart on Wheels.

After two months of this, Sheyene still skates circles around me on the bike path, grinning and flourishing her arms like Tinkerbell sprinkling fairy dust on Franklin Delano Roosevelt in his wheelchair. Nevertheless, each day we increase my distance: to the edge of Santa Monica, to the second public restroom, then the third, and eventually all the way to the Santa Monica pier. And back.

Without falling.

"I've achieved mediocrity!" I declare to Sheyene one day on our way back from the pier.

When I don't fall on my ass in the next five seconds, she replies: "Yes, sweetie, I believe you have."

By the time we return, I've bladed about three miles without falling. I decide to skate the last two blocks down Speedway, simply because the surface there is rougher and more difficult to negotiate. Even so, I do not fall. The cross street in front of our apartment building slopes about five degrees, though, and I'm still not ready for that. So I grab hold of the blue dumpster behind Phoenix House and ease myself down on my butt right there. Success!

Before I can peel off my blades, Sheyene tells me to wait, then rushes upstairs to our apartment. A minute later she returns with a camera and takes my picture. Eventually, the photo will wind up on the web site of Antioch University Los Angeles, where I teach. In the months and years ahead, students will occasionally startle me by declaring that one reason they chose Antioch over other schools was this picture. "Antioch seemed like it would be more fun," they'll say.

But I know none of that as I sit here on the asphalt next to the dumpster, basking in the hard-earned triumph of mediocrity. Instead, I think about what my father, a man who worked with his hands his entire life, would have said about me learning to rollerblade: *It's a totally useless skill, son.*

Sam Hamod

Letter to Lorca, Neruda and Borges

I have seen the stones
of darkness
that hard path
we so seldom want to walk,
but they cannot
encircle me
or my life, for
each moment
of my breath
speaks against
this darkness that we all know
shall someday come, instead
each kiss from apples of spring,
orange blossoms
smelling of you, the
softness of your hands
and the way you smile,
help me build walls
against this darkness, this
caped thing
who comes, cane-in-hand
directing bodies

into darkness, but with
these words
I challenge death,
stand my ground, say,
"Yes, but not for awhile,
not while I have this
moment to love, to feel
to speak"—
 no matter when is when
I'm sure
I'll never be willing to leave...

Victor Rangel-Ribeiro

Growing Old on Two Continents: Some Reflections on Intimations of Immortality

"I have an idea that some men are born out of their due place," wrote Somerset Maugham in *The Moon and Sixpence*. "Accident has cast them amid certain surroundings, but they have always a nostalgia for a home they know not... Perhaps it is this sense of strangeness that sends men far and wide in the search for something permanent, to which they may attach themselves... Sometimes a man hits upon a place to which he mysteriously feels that he belongs. Here is the home he sought, and he will settle amid scenes that he has never seen before, among men he has never known, as though they were familiar to him from his birth. Here at last he finds rest."

The Nobel laureate Rabindranath Tagore had a different take on human migration. In *A Flight of Swans* he writes:

I hear the countless voices of the human heart
Flying unseen,
From the dim past to the dim unblossomed
future....
The void of the universe is resounding with the
music of wings:
'Not here, not here, somewhere far beyond.'

Actually, it was neither Maugham's "nostalgia for a place they know not" nor Tagore's ceaseless quest for "somewhere far beyond" that led me and my wife and baby daughter to leave Bombay for America a half-century ago; rather, it was a simple invitation that my sister Lyra who lived in New York had extended to us: since my young wife was already a quite brilliant pianist, and had concertized in Bombay, why did the two of us not come to New York for a year or two, so she could study at Juilliard and perfect her art? We accepted gladly, but the voyage was fraught with incident: President Nasser of Egypt sealed the Suez Canal days after we had passed through, a storm battered us in the Mediterranean the following day, and a ship foundered behind us even as we made for safety in the Straits of Sicily. Mother Nature did her best to make amends; Mount Etna went into a spectacular eruption as the ship was rolling by, and the captain changed course to give us a better view. The transatlantic crossing in the gigantic *Queen Elizabeth I* was equally stormy; it was a relief to finally make it safely into New York harbor, and realize for the first time that the buildings known as skyscrapers really scraped the skies. On boarding ship in Bombay we had had no intention of settling permanently in the United States; once we arrived, however, and found ourselves surrounded by a lively musical and art scene and a vibrant literary milieu, Lea and I did get the feeling that "here we will settle"; for us, it was also "somewhere far beyond." But the actual decision to settle was made much later.

In retrospect it seems as if our trip to the United States had been preordained. What else could have led a total stranger years earlier to twice knock on my door at the *National Standard* in Bombay, offering to tell me my future? As a skeptical editorial writer I turned him down, but he was most persuasive. "Maharajas pay me a lakh of rupees to read their palms," he told me, "and I'm offering to do it for you for nothing. Why not hear what I have to tell you?" He was a man already in his fifties, so I owed him some respect; besides, if maharajas were willing to pay him a hundred thousand rupees a throw, and it would cost me nothing, the least I could do was hear him out. He studied my palm intently before saying anything, and then when he finally spoke I wished he hadn't. "You think you are going to be married soon," he said. (That was true; I was then in hot pursuit of Lea, a young woman I had fallen madly in love with from afar and at first sight; in the intervening years I had met her and her parents, she had met mine, and all the signs were favorable.) "But the marriage won't happen," the palm reader said. "You'll be going away soon to a distant city. You will come back, and then you will get married. Two years after that you and your wife will go overseas." I smiled and thanked him; we chatted briefly, and he left. As the swinging doors closed behind his back, I thought: There goes a Class A faker...

That was in late October, 1952. At year's end the *Times of India* made me an offer I could not refuse, and come January I was off on a train bound for far-off Calcutta. All thought of wedding plans had to be postponed. But within a year I was back in Bombay, and Lea and I were at last married on September 18, 1954. Exactly one year and eleven months later, on August 15, 1956, my wife and I and our eleven-month-old daughter Eva landed in New York. Can you imagine? That foolish palm reader had been off by a whole 28 days! Worse, he had merely forecast that we would be going overseas, completely missing the fact that we would be going to New York; he had also missed knowing that Lea and I would have a baby and would be taking her with us! Did I call him a faker? Charlatan!

Thinking back farther still, it seems as though my parents had unknowingly begun preparing us for our lives in America while my sister and I were little children. My four siblings and I had been born in a small village in Goa, which was then Portuguese India, and raised in another village in the same territory. Ours was an intercultural family, and we grew up speaking fluent English, Portuguese, and Konkani, the local language. Music came naturally, because my father was an accomplished musician and composer, and our house was filled with music. As a toddler I heard excerpts from Italian opera being performed live in our living room, along with songs by Jerome Kern, Cole Porter, and George Gershwin. The performers included my older sisters and brother and other local talent. Perhaps more significantly, my father also played Sousa marches on the piano and the marimba; "Stars and Stripes Forever" was at the top of his list. And there's more: for being head of their class in almost every subject, the prizes that my siblings gathered by the armful at the village high school (student population just around 200) included classics from England as well as books by Twain, Stowe, and others. I was reading them all, avidly, by the time I was in third grade.

Thus Lea and I experienced no culture shock when we walked off the ship that sunny day in August. Since there were so few Indians around in those days, most of the New Yorkers we met were curious about us; many were warm and welcoming; others were on their guard. The shock we felt was of a different, more serious kind: we found we had left a young and vibrant democracy where wide-ranging political discussions were the norm, only to land in the world's oldest democracy while it was still living under the cloud of McCarthyism. If in the course of a political discussion we expressed our views too freely, we were met with just one snarled response: "Why don't you go back where you came from?" In time I learned to parry that thrust and to counterthrust with "I'm an American Indian. Why don't you go back?" Of course I spoke with forked tongue while keeping a straight face, but it did lead to moments of stunned silence and some introspection.

At the time in May of 1971 that my father at age 90 lay dying in Porvorim of a stroke, I was running a well-known music antiquariat in mid-Manhattan. Some of the world's greatest musicians were my regular customers, but mine was strictly a man-and-a-half operation; to have closed my doors without warning and gone down to Goa would have spelt financial ruin. Leonor and Camila, my two oldest sisters who lived in India and were already by my father's bedside, advised me not to come; they said my father was hallucinating and would not recognize me; and even had he been lucid, they said, he himself would have urged me not to come. My father died on May 11; their words salved my conscience but did not ease my pain.

Following local custom, the body was kept on view in the family home's great hall and then taken in procession first to the local chapel and then to the church cemetery, some four miles away. My brother flew down from Geneva and so did my sister from Queens. Thus, all four of my siblings formed part of the funeral procession whose hundreds of mourners included Goa's elite as well as the poorest of the poor. I'm told that when the head of the procession reached the ornate sixteenth-century village chapel, a thousand feet farther along the country lane, the tail end was just leaving our house.

In July I was finally able to leave my antiquariat in safe hands for a month and fly down with my wife and two children to pay our own final homage to the man we loved and revered but was now two months gone. By then the monsoon was venting its fury. We flew from New York to Bombay, then took the train to Goa, a journey that took more than a day. As the meter-gauge train tunneled down the mountains on to the plains we saw that the monsoon had wrought its magic —the landscape was a tapestry of shades of green such as our children had never seen before.

The final tortuous thirty kilometers home by taxi involved our being ferried across two major rivers before the cab finally climbed up to the Porvorim plateau, where a few low houses now lined an area where only jackals had roamed when I was a child. When the road looped down into the village I saw that little else had changed. The right turn into our lane was as sharp and as treacherous as it had always been; as the car lurched between the chapel on the left and a cousin's maternity hospital on the right, pedestrians had to flatten themselves against one wall or the other. Another right turn, and we were passing our tenants' houses; and then, beyond our garden wall, the façade of our centuries-old house itself came into view, half-hidden by mango and cashew trees. Children who had been playing in the lane now ran ahead of the cab, racing us. When we stopped at the wrought iron gate they came back, to stand around and gawk. My oldest sister Leonor, twelve years my senior, rushed out to greet us; Camila had gone back to Bombay. Our joy was immense; why then were tears coursing down our cheeks?

I had been born in that house and it was pretty much as I remembered it. The garden gate still creaked, obviating the need for a bell by the main door. One passed between beds of roses and then climbed a flight of broad steps that led to the *balcão*, the broad pillared porch, open on three sides, that served as an informal meeting place and also gave access to the interior. A mountain stream, swollen by the monsoon rains, burbled on the far side; I knew without looking that now it would be teeming with tiny fish, and that frogs would be out each night, reciting their version of the rosary.

As we followed Leonor inside, the children marveled at the centuries' old interior walls, each more than a foot thick, at the broad expanse of the main hall, at the height of its ceiling that soared up more than twenty feet; at the windows that instead of glass panes had strips of translucent shells placed between vertical wooden slats to let in a suffused light.

No sooner had we arrived than we began to receive a steady trickle of visitors. Some were relatives; others were neighbors, still others were *mundkars*—tenant farmers and village craftsmen—who lived rent free on our properties and were stopping by to pay their condolences and their respects to the man who, along with his wife and his siblings, was their new *bhatkar*, their landlord.

One of the last to come at around five in the evening was an old man, perhaps not quite seventy years of age. The confident way he opened the gate and walked up the steps told me he was a familiar; his children and I had probably played together as kids, but I had left the village long ago and only been back so sporadically that I did not recognize him. However, Leonor told me who he was: Baboni, the master carpenter, whose humble house lay just beyond our compound. I rose and greeted him warmly.

What followed next took me by surprise. "I dandled you on my knee when you were a baby," he said, speaking softly in Konkani but with great intensity. "You would come to our house and we would feed you sweets. Where were you when your father died? Your brother and sister came down from Europe and America. We were waiting for you by the roadside, but you were nowhere to be seen. What kept you there?" His heartfelt words reopened a wound and forced me to reexamine my conscience. Could I have found a way out of my dilemma? Had I tried hard enough to find one? Baboni spoke for long minutes, and standing beside me my wife took in everything he said; our children understood not a word, and yet knew what was going on: their father was being bawled out by someone whose station in life was far enough below ours that he should have known better, but though their father was feeling the pain, he was not fighting back.

When Baboni had finished I accepted his rebuke without trying to justify myself. Instead, I thanked him for having spoken so frankly, and for the love and loyalty he had shown my father down the years. We sat and chatted awhile, about his family and mine; when he stood up to go he asked my wife for the gift of a piece of cloth. We gladly gave him some and he went on his way. My daughter Eva, aged 16, and son Eric, aged 12, were ready with a question: Baboni was our tenant, who lived on our land rent-free; he depended on us, not we on him. Why then, they wanted to know, did I put up with his anger and his scolding?

I told them that Baboni had known me and cared for me when I was a little child, and I felt his rebuke was justified.

"Still," Eva said, "he had no right to speak to you like that."

It was time to let my US-raised children in on another truth: In India, as in so much of the Old World, when it's a matter of commanding respect and attention, age trumps status, especially when one holds the moral high ground.

Lea and I lay awake that night, unused to the stillness that the croaking of the frogs only served to intensify. With no electricity and no streetlights the room was in pitch darkness but through tiny cracks in the roof tiles we caught hints of starlight. My sister lay asleep in an adjoining bedroom. My father's presence was everywhere.

My father's own age as well as his social status had no doubt weighed on several minds some ten years before this incident, when in December of 1961 the Indian Army had rolled across the frontier of what was then still a foreign colony. Wishing to avoid a futile loss of life, Gen. Vassalo e Silva, the Portuguese Governor-General, had ordered his troops to offer no resistance, and they swirled back before the advancing forces like leaves before an autumn wind. Word came that Indian troops advancing from the north were rapidly approaching Mapusa, the provincial capital just five miles from Porvorim; to get from there to the capital city of Panjim they would have to take the road that cut right through our village. Our panicked villagers needed someone who would intercede on their behalf, and rather than turn to the local sheriff-cum-mayor, or *regedor*, they turned to my father. Oscar Rangel Ribeiro at 80 may well have figured that though the Indian officers would care nothing at all about his social standing, they would certainly spot the gray in his beard, so he picked up his walking stick and planted himself at the spot where the main road intersected our country lane. Fortunately, the armored column leading the thrust had heard that the road had been mined, and took a different route, so we can only speculate on what would have happened when an irresistible force finally confronted a highly movable object who showed no fear.

My father was 44 years old when I was born in 1925, yet I never regarded him as an old man, perhaps because he never acted the part. When I was eleven and he was fifty-five we all lived in the village of Saligao, and I remember that in the evenings we played as partners in a doubles badminton game where our opponents were the principal and vice-principal of the local elementary school. The badminton court lay directly across the road from our house, and I realize now that in those games I played the role of being my father's partner as well as his chaperone, because he was a handsome man with a roving eye, and the principal and vice-principal we played against, though ungainly and fat, were both women. This caused my mother considerable anxiety, and I remember one night at dinner when a tureen flung across the table missed him by a whisker. However, their marriage held solidly together, and was ended only by my mother's untimely death in 1954. They had been married 42 years.

Some months before the Portuguese were ousted he visited us in our apartment in Forest Hills, New York. While we chatted I pulled out a plank I was going to saw by hand to make a shelf for a bookcase. He grabbed the saw out of my hand and insisted on doing the job himself; being an excellent craftsman, he did a much better job of it than I could have. This man of so many parts, what couldn't he do? He's been dead thirty-six years and I still live in his shadow...

That same year on returning to Goa he began building my oldest sister a house up on the Porvorim plateau, supervising the construction himself. His letters kept us informed of developments. "The sun gets quite hot even by 11 in the morning," he wrote to us that summer. "The heat does not bother me. But by midday I begin to feel tired, a bit weak at the knees, and I can't understand why."

His boundless energy made me, in Shakespeare's words, "insensible of mortality, and desperately mortal." As long as he was alive he stood a strong bulwark between Death and me; once that rampart was struck down, I was forced to confront the inevitability of my own passing. He, too, must have had similar thoughts when, while visiting us on a couple of occasions, he got news of the death of a beloved sibling; he retired quietly to his room, where I found him seated on his bed, absorbed in his thoughts and in prayer. Never deeply religious in his early years, even anti-clerical at times, with advancing age he turned his thoughts to the hereafter. I now regret that somehow we never got around to talking about it.

Today we live much longer than Charles Lamb's generation did when, in 1798 and at the age of only twenty-three, he lamented that all, all are gone, the old familiar faces. We are also a much more mobile society, and this is one more reason why our loneliness increases as we age: We lose touch, and we try to re-establish touch, but often when we reach out our hands find only emptiness. In the 1960s I conducted a small chamber orchestra I had founded in Queens; we met once a week for a couple of hours, and made marvelous music together, playing Bach and Beethoven, Bloch and Bartok, as much as lay within our powers. Some years after we disbanded, I wanted to share a thought with my former concertmaster, and dialed his number. A woman answered. I asked to speak to Aldo Regis, and she was instantly suspicious—and hostile. "Who are you?" she wanted to know. "What do you want? Why do you want to speak to Aldo?" I learnt then to my embarrassment that Aldo had died months earlier.

Shortly thereafter I got an urge to phone Emanuel Balaban, my first conducting teacher, who had been a conductor with the Ballet Russe de Montecarlo and had taught at Juilliard. I dialed his number and found it had been disconnected; he too had passed away. A week later I was in a bus rolling down Lexington Avenue and on passing St. Peter's Lutheran Church at 53rd Street had an irresistible impulse to get off and go see the organist Gordon Jones. He had spent time in India during World War II, and been a special customer of mine at the music store; we had become fast friends. When I asked for him at the desk the receptionist burst into tears; she told me he had walked in from the street just days earlier, sat beside her apparently to catch his breath, and passed away from a heart attack before her very eyes. From that time on, whenever I got the urge to contact one friend or another, I wondered whether that was a sign the friend had died. I was afraid to call, and afraid not to call. Eventually I turned that fear and uncertainty into a short story.

It seems to be universally true that as we grow older we men tend to turn our minds to higher things; some of us try to figure out what awaits us in the hereafter; yet others think in more worldly terms and consult lawyers to help protect their estates; others still focus on how best to bridge the widening gap between east and west—should they comb those wispy strands of hair from left to right, or would it be better the other way around?

What goes on in our heads determines how we spend our lives. Which brings us now to words that were spoken not twenty years but twenty-four centuries ago: Socrates' challenge to all of us, that we should examine our lives, or find too late that they have not been worth living. In 1941, when I was a sixteen-year-old freshman in St. Xavier's College in Bombay, our Spanish Jesuit principal defined that challenge for several of us in terms that were far tougher: "You should not just examine your lives, you should examine your lives every day," he said. "Each night, as you prepare to go to sleep, ask yourselves three questions: How have I, today, touched the life of someone I know? How have I touched the life of someone I don't know? And lastly, what have I done today to improve on the talents that God has given me?" If you can't answer positively to any one of those questions, the good Fr. Coyne said to us, do not go to sleep until you have set that right. Most members of our group were so impressed that we have tried to follow his advice to this day, and many are the sleepless nights we have spent as a result....

Late in 2004 my wife and I made a transition in our lives

as significant as our initial move from India to the United States. Psychologically, for us it was a more difficult decision, but our hands were forced: in January of that year, while Lea and I were in India, our home in New York, that we had lived in for 42 years, was destroyed by bursting water pipes. In considering our options we decided we would never move into an "adult community," where residents have to be 55 or older in order to buy a house, and children are allowed only as visitors. As fate would have it, the most attractive house we could find, and the one that best suited our needs, was in an adult community in New Jersey. We talked ourselves into buying it, on the grounds that our daughter and her children in Princeton would be just twenty minutes away, and our son and his family in Virginia two hours closer to us than they had previously been. Surprise! Our too-adult neighbors surrounding us have proven themselves to be a truly vibrant group, friendly, culturally involved, and intellectually stimulating.

Each winter, the snowbirds among them fly south to Florida; we fly east to Europe and India. And we then spend at least four months in our ancestral home in Goa, thanks to the fact that in 2001 Lea retired from her post as principal at the UN International School in New York, a post she had held for 32 years. Our relatives in Goa number in the hundreds, and they treat us with great respect. As I am one of the oldest members of this extended family and Lea is not far behind, protocol demands that we not be called by our first names, American style, but by our name always preceded by an honorific. Thus I am addressed as "Primo Vitor" (Cousin Victor); Lea is "Prima Lea." Contrast that with the joyous shout and wave with which my grandson in Princeton greeted me when I visited him on his third birthday: "Hi, Vic!" (Now he calls me 'Grandpa'.)

Once we are ensconced in our ancestral Goan village, from time to time we hire a taxi and drive a jagged course towards the setting sun, until we reach famed Calangute beach. As a child I would ride there in the family's creaky wooden carriage, drawn by a pair of well-trained bullocks; we had to get off and walk whenever the incline proved to be too steep. The twelve-mile trip that used to take about two hours now takes just a fraction of the time. And there is one other difference: where once as a child I frolicked thigh-deep in swirling water, daring the waves to knock me down even as I scampered away from them, I am now content to stand serenely at the water's edge, wearing the bottoms of my trousers rolled. The mighty breakers thunder and crash a hundred yards away; it is only the privileged foam that gets to kiss my toes.

Consider now the paradox of age: the world's population is getting younger even as it is growing older. The cult of youth is changing in the United States: to be forty was once considered being "over the hill"; now thirty is the dividing line between achievement and possible failure. The youth in India have adapted the same attitude, and with that much ferment in so many millions of young people that nation is on the move.

That said, I must admit that people our age in both cultures are now more active than ever before. Whether they are involved in the arts, the sciences, politics, community development or social work, senior citizens in droves have been getting off their rocking chairs in order to make a difference. To what do we owe this burst of energy? Perhaps the notion has spread that old age, far from being a liability, is the culmination and reward for a life well spent; perhaps more of us, having examined our lives, determine to spend our remaining time as joyously and productively as possible. Just such a point was made in a "Broadway show" staged by residents of our adult community last night. Hit songs and dance numbers from disparate shows had been strung together for the evening; though the singers were sometimes off-key, and the dancers less than professional, such was their verve and joie de vivre that we in the audience enjoyed ourselves thoroughly. Certainly for the scores of performers and the vast and wildly applauding audience of senior citizens the most poignant and relevant lines were those we and the

chorus so lustily sang at the end—
Make this moment last,
Because the best of times is now, is now, is now.

Although a veil prevents us from directly seeing what lies beyond the purely physical world, William James speaks of "the reality behind the veil." We have hearsay evidence of that reality, of the possible existence of a spirit world, which we may or may not believe, depending on how far we are removed from the source. That reality also varies depending on time and place. For example, in the early years of the twentieth century all of Porvorim knew the story of the woman who had been bewitched and disappeared in the night, only to be found next morning sitting on the tip of the topmost branch of a tall tamarind tree. That tree grew not fifty yards from our front gate, and as a child I was shown the very branch on whose feathery tip the woman had been seated. It was said that Catholic priests had been called to exorcise her and had failed; but when a Hindu priest was called, he lit a pot of incense at the base of the trunk, and when the smoke and the fumes swirled up to where the woman inhaled them, the tree bent over and gently lowered her to the ground. The village is now more than ninety per cent literate, and were I to tell the story now, few would believe it, except perhaps for some very old people who as children had heard the story themselves from their own parents or grandparents.

It is harder by far to disbelieve a first-hand account provided by someone who is near and dear to us. My father often told us how, walking home one moonlit night from a far-off village, he took a familiar short cut, and found himself in the middle of a vast field that was bathed in mist, with cattle grazing on all sides; the cold dampness of the mist settling on his head and neck was tempered by the heat rising from the cattle. He threaded his way in between the peacefully grazing animals, feeling no fear, and it was only when he found himself clear of the herd and back on the road that he realized how unusual the experience had been, for cattle are never put out to pasture at night, and would not have been left untended. So he turned to look, and saw only a barren field, and the dim contours of the winding path he had walked along; of the animals and the mist there was no trace. Perturbed, he revisited the site next morning, looking for some tangible traces of what he had experienced; he found none.

My own experience of the "reality behind the veil" occurred in the first week of July, 2002, and was much more personal. I had just undergone a quadruple bypass in a New York hospital, and because my heart muscle was extraordinarily strong, the surgeon had bypassed the heart-lung machine, and worked on my beating heart. All went well. That night, however, I began to shiver uncontrollably, and was given a quick blood transfusion. With my wife and my sister spending the night huddled on chairs in the nearby waiting room, I spent the night alone, and not alone; twice during the night, when sharp pain jolted me awake, I felt the comforting presence of two beings who had passed away just months earlier—my beloved mother-in-law Cecilia Vaz, who had died in May 2000, and my sister Leonor, who had died in October 2001. Each time, I saw no one in the darkened room, yet they were there, I felt them right there by the bed, and I went back to sleep feeling warm, strengthened, and secure. I was home, mending rapidly, three days later. Mine was not a near-death experience; I saw no blinding light, heard no voice telling me to go back; yet, having for long kept an open mind as to whether or not there is life after death, now I am convinced there is.

Thinking back now to that incident, which for me was so real, I realize that the veil separating the physical and the spiritual worlds acts very much like the double lines that separate opposing lines of traffic on our streets and highways—the dotted line abuts the spirit world, the solid white line is on our side. The traffic rules remain the same: they can thus cross into our reality and our life at will; we can only cross into their world when we die. Some of us are more eager to cross than others, especially when severe illness strikes and the pain is intense and unbearable. Yet others go suddenly for no obvious reason, often these include people who have set themselves a goal that to them will be the crowning event of their lives and who die soon after they have achieved it. Is it, as the popular phrase goes, that "their time had come," or did they just consciously let go of life? Perhaps they did, but I believe that most of us would rather go tomorrow than today, for noble or for very personal reasons. Bakibab Borkar, a poet who is little known in this country but much loved in Goa, penned this personal appeal to Yamma, the God of Death:

Please, Sir, Mr. God of Death,
Don't make it my turn today.
Not today, Sir…
We have fish curry for dinner.

Since in Goa one has fish curry for dinner more often than not, Bakibab lived on to write more poems. Biographers have neglected to note what curry Bakibab was feasting on, the night Yamma finally came to call.

My own first encounter with the concepts of both infinity and eternity came when, as a child of nine, I had a fractured forearm reset. Ether had been used as the anesthetic; as a result, I suffered recurring nightmares, in which a brilliant pinpoint of light appeared in a black night sky; circles of light sprang from this center and pulsed outwards out of sight. The thought that these ripples of light were coursing through the universe, and that the universe had no limit, terrified me; I could not imagine what my afterlife would be in a universe so frighteningly immense. My mother said I should consult Fr. Bellarmino, the gruff and burly priest who taught religion in our school; though during class he relied on a cane to drive home the trickier points in dogma, he talked to me gently, assuring me that in the next life God's love would so envelop all of us that the size of the universe would not matter one bit. The nightmares stopped.

Thoughts of a hereafter again entered my head with my father's death some forty years later. Remembering vaguely that Socrates during his trial had had a thing or two to say about death and the afterlife, I felt he might be worth listening to. So I looked him up in Plato, rather than looking him up on Google, and found that Socrates, after telling his judges that "no one knows whether death ... may not be the greatest good," had gone on to utter an even more positive statement: "Be of good cheer about death, and know of a certainty, that no evil can happen to a good man, either in life or after death." Though he quoted no source for that belief, that was indeed a comforting pronouncement, especially since I, like most of my fellows, regard myself as being "a good man." But at the end of his speech Socrates also said: "The hour of departure has arrived, and we go our ways—I to die, and you to live. Which is better God only knows." So when he had so categorically stated, scant seconds earlier, that a good man has nothing to fear after death, he—misspoke? Ouch!

The priests and the prophets are more consistent, assuring us that there will indeed be an afterlife, where we will face the judgment of God and be allotted either the bliss of heaven or the tortures of hell. Down the centuries this has caused anxiety to both president and plebeian. Billy Graham recently told *TIME Magazine* that President Eisenhower had asked him repeatedly for an answer to the question: how can people really know that they are going to heaven? The evangelist confessed that he had had no answer. Eisenhower's question took it for granted that there is in fact a heaven; in this the aging warrior joined the vast majority of mankind, the common men who, William James wrote, "have interpolated divine miracles into the field of nature, they have built a heaven out beyond the grave." And they have done this—and here I am juxtaposing another of his statements—because "immortality is one of the great spiritual needs of man." Prospects of heaven and immortality are thus the twin carrots that help us get through life.

Perhaps Billy Graham could have both sidestepped and

answered the president's question by reminding him of something an itinerant young rabbi had said to the Pharisees who questioned him after he had come down to Jerusalem from the windswept hillsides of Samaria and Galilee. They asked him when the kingdom of God would come down to earth—which, when you think about it, is the reverse of the question that plagued Dwight Eisenhower in our own time. And the rabbi said to them, in effect, 'you will not be able to see it, and say, It is here! It is there! For the kingdom of heaven is within you.' Those words resonate today perhaps even more than when they were first spoken all those centuries ago. In all of the Bible, I take that one statement literally, and what a wonderful statement it is. The theological implications are both ego-building and ego-shattering, because now at one and the same time I hold the key to heaven in my hands but it is no longer exclusively mine to hold. Further, there is no longer any compulsion for me to convert you in order to save you, and to kill you if you refuse to convert, since the kingdom of heaven is already in you as it is in me.

Think now of the impact on society: If we live our lives holding to that belief, and our actions towards our fellowmen are rooted in it, we will be fair and just to all in all our dealings, and live our lives in peace and contentment. Whatever then happens after death is totally irrelevant. We will have enjoyed heaven on earth while alive, and if there is yet a greater heaven when we close our eyes for the very last time on earth, what a grand bonus that will be!

Victor Rangel-Ribeiro

The Old Man and the Sea

When I consider how my days are spent
   On this broad beach, watching the waters wide
   On whose bold billows soaring surfers ride
While I but stand, bereft of all intent
To crouch on bucking board with both knees bent
   Lest a rude wipeout wipe out all my pride —
   Ah, could I but breast th'incoming tide
Just once again, to stem my discontent!

Swept by the wind a curling comber grows.
   I watch a surge of surfers paddle in vain
     To catch it ere it breaks. Their hopes betray'd,
They skulk. The spent wave warms my toes,
   Spritzing a soothing message from the mighty main:
     They also surf, who only stand and wade.

Robert Gover

A Motorized Life

So here I go zooming down the interstate, marveling that not many decades ago we humans only dreamed of skimming over the surface of Mother Earth, like birds swooping. Maybe I'm driving the last car I'll ever own. Maybe not. It's 2006 and I'm 76. Even though I feel pretty good, there are all those insidious advertisements that say, "See your doctor, take this pill, reserve your cemetery plot, check your life insurance," and those that portray a spiffy new car like an old man's substitute for a new love affair.

I think of past cars I've owned and how each is associated with a period in my life. The one I drive now is a 1997 Acura RL. The engine sounds good, the interior is like new, the paint job is holding up, and it needs minimum maintenance. It's in better shape than I am. I have a gimpy left knee that needs "reconstruction." My car needs no reconstruction, just an oil change now and then, and new tires every few years. It's so surprisingly durable it threatens to outlive me.

First car I ever owned was a 1940 Plymouth in 1951. I was in college when a friend joined the Air Force to avoid the Korean War draft. Mac first loaned me his car while he was away, then signed it over to me free and clear when he decided to make the Air Force his career. How liberating to own a car! I soon christened the back seat with a cute honey and drove that baby (the car) till she quit one beautiful day in May on the Pennsylvania Turnpike, about halfway between Pittsburgh and Philadelphia. I'd been driving to the Jersey shore to work as a lifeguard over the summer. Had to abandon that car and hitchhike.

I was on an athletic scholarship and had developed the habit of signing up for twice as many courses as I needed then dropping those I didn't like, and I'd dropped so many that after four years I still needed a semester more to get a degree. So I got a job in a steel mill and, for $100, bought a 1939 Chevy to commute. It used more oil than gas, but that was okay because part of my job was to throw away the used oil from company trucks, so I threw a crankcase worth into that old Chevy each working day. As I commuted to the job, I passed a trolley island at the bottom of a long hill and when I gunned the Chevy to climb the next hill, it emitted such a huge cloud of black smoke the people on the Trolley Island disappeared. Got so the people on the island recognized this smokepot coming and scurried back to the sidewalk. I wanted to stop and apologize but that wouldn't have solved the problem.

I associate this jalopy with a difficult period after I got my diploma and quit the mill job, was living on unemployment and working on a series of short stories, collecting rejections and fearful of starving. My fiancée became so exasperated she dumped me. For about a year I was pouring short stories into the mail almost as fast as oil into the Chevy. I kept wishing the thing would quit so I'd be forced to get another car but it just kept smoke-potting along.

Fast-forward to my first "real" job: sports editor of a small daily in upstate Pennsylvania. I was resigned to bird-dogging used oil forever when the local banker asked why I didn't buy a new car and, if I liked their fair town, even buy a house and settle down there, Greenville. Seems only a moment later the Ford dealer collared me and put me into a brand new 1954 white and blue Fairlane. I now had a girlfriend who lived about 90 miles away, so once a week, then two or three times a week, I'd take off in the Fairlane for her place. Life was good: the town had three football teams—college, public high and Catholic high—and combined they lost only 2 games that season. Going to away games in my spiffy new Fairlane loaded with "helpers" to keep the play-by-play, take photos, provide "comforts," etc. Big fun.

I still drove the Fairlane when I got married (for the first time) at age 25, and became "responsible," by taking a better paying corporate public relations job. My boss said the Ford Fairlane was just the right car for my status in the company but that I had to upgrade my sartorial façade from grubby newspaper reporter to dedicated *Wall Street Journal* reader. The job started to go south when I was required to see the company psychiatrist and take an IQ test. I had minored in psychology at Pitt and fulfilled my lab requirement by giving to 100 students three different IQ tests, so I knew IQ tests like I'd written them myself. I scored exceptionally high and was thereafter viewed by the company brass with a mix of awe and dark suspicion. Simultaneously, the repo man arrived to snatch the Fairlane. I'd forgotten to make payments. I got the money together and hung onto it, even though it was rapidly becoming a mechanic's delight.

I was fired from the PR job for "socialist sympathies." I'd prepared a feature story for the company magazine about a crane operator who'd quit to take the job of his dreams, political cartoonist for the Youngstown (Ohio) *Vindicator*. The cartoon he drew to go with the story showed a mechanical crane lifting a huge bundle of scrap metal with musical notes and the words, "You lift sixteen ton and what do you get." My boss didn't listen to pop music and when he took the magazine's contents into the board meeting, I soon heard loud, angry voices and table thumping.

Getting dumped by the corporation was a blessing in disguise. I collected unemployment compensation and stayed home and wrote: a three-act play and a bunch of short stories. My new wife, Millie, a nurse anesthetist, used the Fairlane to commute. Nothing I wrote sold and I sank into discouragement. Where I got my hair cut, the barber used to say, "Are you working?" meaning did I have a job, and I'd say, "Yes." And he'd say, "Where?" and I'd say, "At home, writing." In his mind, "working" and "at home" were mutually exclusive states of being. When I got another newspaper job, he brightened with the news that I was "working," even though I lamented that I was not working, I was employed.

My first beat in the Ambridge-Aliquippa area was the police stations every morning. The Chief in Aliquippa became my favorite. He'd been born in Estonia and spoke eight languages, and was a collector of weird crime stories. It was easier to hang out with him, drink coffee and listen to his endless crime tales than go back to the office and bang out copy on an old mechanical typewriter.

Aliquippa had been populated by successive waves of immigrants—every time one load of imported workers went out on strike at the local Jones and Laughlin Steel Mill, another was brought in to replace them. The town's neighborhoods were called "Plans." Each Plan contained an ethnic group: Italians here, Serbians there, Ukrainians over yonder, etc. Just when I was becoming fascinated by this American phenomenon, I was reassigned to be the feature writer.

At first I missed hanging out with the Aliquippa Chief but soon adapted, because as feature writer, I didn't have to report to the office every day. I could call up the editor and tell him what feature I had in mind and get a lot of my own writing done meanwhile.

How I became a feature writer had to do with another mode of travel and an aged dude named Mote Bergman. Mote was a birthday walker. On his birthday, he'd go to Atlantic City and walk a mile of boardwalk for every year he'd been alive. I tuned into Mote when I was in my twenties and he in his seventies. Everyone else on the newspaper loathed having to write this annual piece about Mote's birthday walk, but I had fun with it. I had so much fun with it that Mote decided to walk from the Pittsburgh area to New York City when the Pirates played the Yankees in the World Series. Every evening he'd report in by phone and I'd write up his latest day on the road, and the editor would slap it on the front page. By the time he reached the Lincoln Tunnel, a movie producer was interested in making his life story. Mote made a nice hunk of change for the rights to his story but the movie was never made. Well, film captures sights and sounds; Mote's walking was exceedingly mental and tactile.

When it seemed a good idea to trade in the Fairlane I chanced upon a very used Porsche. Back in the 1950s in Western Pennsylvania, people would look at this little thing and say, "Is that a *real* car?" Not only was it a joy to commute in, but I won trophies in various sports car races. I was driving this old Porsche when I wrote *One Hundred Dollar Misunderstanding*. I drove it to New York City to present the manuscript to my agent, Jack Lewis of American Literary Exchange. He'd been trying to shop three other novels I'd written and said I was a "major talent," but after reading OHDM, he fired me, said he would no longer represent me. His partner, Aladar Farkus, shopped the novel behind Jack's back. When it was roundly rejected in the USA, Aladar sent it to Paris, where it was immediately welcomed. The French agent, Serge Ouvaroff, sent me a note declaring it "literature!" It was translated by France's specialist in African American slang, Marcel Duhamel.

There was a lag time of a year or so before the French translation and publication, so it was back to work at another newspaper job, this one in Annapolis, Maryland. The old Porsche had finally quit so I put a down payment on a Karmann Ghia convertible, hung a portable radio from its mirror and sallied forth to cover politics in Maryland's capital, where corruption wasn't a scandal, it was a way of life. I was driving back to the Pittsburgh area weekends in the Ghia with the portable radio swinging from the rearview mirror when a British publisher sent me a contract for OHDM, with a nasty contingency: I had to change "fuck" to "fug" or he would not publish. I negotiated and got him to give me 100 percent of the dramatic rights in return for this silly censorship. But making those changes made me physically ill and took the fun out of driving the

Ghia.

Not long after that I was wintering in a motel just south of Atlantic City, divorced, when a combination full moon, high tide and strong winds sent the Ghia floating down the street in seawater. I had no insurance. I'd again quit a job to write another novel and was on a very tight budget. But quickly on top of this catastrophe came reviews from Paris: they loved OHDM in French translation and called me a "bright comet in an otherwise dark (American) literary sky." Ian Ballantine and his editor Bernard Shir-Cliff came looking for me to offer a contract, then added Grove Press to do the hardback, and I got another payday. The Ghia was traded in on a brand new Oldsmobile Cutlass convertible. The dealer was so fascinated by the Ghia, he didn't even notice that its transmission was making a strange noise. I mentioned that the car had had a little sea voyage but he was so fascinated with the thing, he didn't listen.

My first novel rose up the *New York Times* bestseller list during a citywide printers union strike, which shut down periodical publications, around the time of the Cuban Missile Crisis. When the printers went back to work it was third on the list and I was flat broke, living in an old stone house near Christiana, PA, which had been built before the Revolutionary War. I was alone, and lonely, and chopping wood to stoke the fireplaces to keep warm as autumn turned to winter. The house had no central heating. You either chopped wood or froze. The nearest phone was in my landlady's house, about 70 yards away. Movie producers began to call about obtaining rights to this novel that was causing a buzz. The landlady would fetch me and I'd jog over to her house to answer the calls, which sometimes included invitations to lunch at fancy restaurants in New York City. I'd borrow gas money and drive to Manhattan. I could make it there and back in a day.

An editor at Grove Press advised that I'd best bring an agent with me to these business luncheons, so I got in touch with Jack Lewis, the agent who'd dumped me when he'd first read OHDM.

I would have much preferred Aladar Farkus but his Hungarian-accented English wasn't up to the job. At a luncheon in the St. Regis Hotel, Jack became so flustered by the big dollar numbers being jabbered about by a producer from Universal Studios that I had to escort him outside and hail a cab for him. I wound up in an eight-year legal battle with that producer. He claimed we had a deal. The only written evidence was my note to him saying I did not accept his offer. The case was settled by the New York Supreme Court, which affirmed that I did not accept his offer. For what I paid in legal fees, I could have bought a small fleet of Mercedes.

During this period, I moved with a girlfriend to Vero Beach, Florida, which was then populated mainly by right-wing conservatives from the Midwest. I was avidly following the civil rights movement unfolding in the Deep South at this time and went to Washington to hear Martin Luther King's famous "I have a dream" speech. On the edge of Vero Beach was Gifford, the "black" side of town. I became a member of the Gifford Chapter of the NAACP and began hanging out with a like-minded member, seven-foot-tall Alfonso Moran. One Saturday night while Alfonso and I were playing a spirited game of eight ball, the police arrived in the bar and arrested about a dozen men, including Alfonso. I learned that this was part of the community routine. They'd arrest these guys Saturday night and release them pending payment of bail, to be made as they worked picking oranges the following week, at the end of which they'd be arrested again and again ordered to pay bail from their labors the following week. I wrote an article about this which was published in a New York "leftist" weekly, which somehow got reprinted and circulated in Vero Beach, which led to the night I almost wound up at the bottom of Indian River in a cement casket. I was alerted by Wendell Harris, an ACLU lawyer in Vero—we'd become friends and he had a "plant" on the inside of the right-wing group, who picked up the news that "citizens" were on their way to my house to make a "citizens' arrest," and that some of them were mixing the cement casket in preparation for terminating me. I grabbed a toothbrush and hopped in my Olds convertible and didn't stop driving till I was in Manhattan.

I was introduced to the novelist James Baldwin, who'd recently scored a coup with his *New Yorker Magazine* article, "The Fire Next Time." Jimmy strongly advised that I move to Europe. I thought seriously about this, but procrastinated due to another lawsuit—this one trans-Atlantic, concerning royalties owed me by the British publisher.

Soon I was living in an apartment in New York City, where housing a car costs as much as housing a human, so I sold the Olds to Hertz in return for rental credits. Nelson Algren came to New York and I hosted him and his lady in my apartment. He was involved in a trans-Atlantic lawsuit to recover the movie rights to *Man With the Golden Arm*, stolen from him by a producer who lived in London. Nelson used money from sales of his other best-selling novel, *Walk on the Wild Side* to mount his trans-Atlantic lawsuit. When his money ran out, his New York and London lawyers stopped working. He passed away without recovering his stolen property.

I stayed in the USA and developed a taste for big cars (just when the VW bug was gaining popularity) so when I found myself living in Malibu because my novels were sparking interest from movieland, I bought a big Olds 98. I ran around with Jim Morrison of The Doors about this time and he loved to drive that thing, would snatch the keys from my fingers and lizard himself behind the wheel. The Doors were on the cusp of what was to become a huge success and Jim seemed a bit disoriented. I was into wife number 3 by this point (I didn't always get permission from church or state for my matrimonial adventures) and we'd wake up some mornings to find Jim asleep on the living room couch, our fruit bowl and liquor supply greatly depleted. When he asked me to accompany The Doors on their European tour, I respectfully declined. Jim was like two people: sober Jim the quiet recluse in the corner, drunk Jim the daredevil toying with death. He was a tremendously talented poet and I knew he was going to become a legend, but hanging out with him was hard, unrewarding work.

I landed a three-book deal from a big publisher—they paid me the biggest advance ever made to an American novelist—and bought the car I'd dreamed about years ago: a Mercedes sports two-seater, brand new in 1968. This car became my all-time favorite, even though it was to deliver lessons in humility. It came out of merges onto freeways with such thrust it got me a rash of speeding tickets. It zigged and zagged through tight traffic like a Heisman Trophy halfback through a crowd of would-be tacklers. So here I was living on top of the proverbial hog with a net worth of over $1M and feeling like I'd come a long way, baby, from the orphanage I'd grown up in. One day I tried to zigzag through a traffic jam on the 101 in Santa Barbara and wound up rolling the Mercedes several times before it came to a stop, the hardtop down below the steering wheel and me on the floor hugging the gear shift. If I'd had my seatbelt fastened that day, I'd have been worm food.

Around this time my editor got handed his head in a corporate merger and the new editor was a merchant prince with a medieval mindset. The same week *Publisher's Weekly Magazine* showcased the cover of my upcoming novel *Poorboy at the Party* on its cover, this merchant prince told me, "We're going to cut your contract." I said, "That's illegal!" He smiled and said, "So sue." My agent said, "Don't sue, run. They have your life insured for eight million, and you could have, like, an accident." After sending out review copies, this publisher sent out notice that publication had been cancelled. A few months later a notice followed that publication had not been canceled but postponed. The first printing was cut from 50,000 copies down to 5,000, "proving" that this novel was not a hot seller.

I moved to Europe and drove a series of rented Fiats till the life insurance policy lapsed and was not renewed.

Back in the USA, while driving from New York City to

California, I swung through southern Kentucky to check out the area where my father had come from, and stopped for gas just outside the small town of Monticello. When I handed the African American proprietor my credit card, he laughed and said, "That's my name." He was the Robert Gover I'd played with during summers when my mother had sent me to get acquainted with my father's people. We had a good time recalling hoeing tobacco and gathering cannon balls from field and forest to stack on my great-grandfather's lawn. During the Civil War, Yankee gunboats had steamed up the Cumberland River and tried to shell the main house but all their shots fell short. This Robert Gover was like an Africanized version of me, and I an Anglicized version of him, reminding us both that, for people with roots in colonial America, racial purity is a color-blurred hallucination.

A few years later, I went shopping for my next car with my six-year-old son, who helped a salesman persuade me to buy a 1972 Mazda sedan. It was utilitarian and held up till I returned from a trip to Brazil, researching African American pantheism for my book *Voodoo Contra*. It was steadfastly rejected by major publishers. As one editor put it, "What you need to do is drop the religious philosophy and get a snake crawling up the body of a naked woman tied to a stake, write a scary novel about it." The book was declared "mysticism" and published in condensed form by Samuel Weiser Company of York Beach, Maine.

I lamented that I seemed always to be swimming against the cultural beliefs—a satire on miscegenation, a serious examination of that scary awesome word *voodoo*, and by then research into historical economic turning points and the cycles of the slower, outermost planets. As though in sync with my mood at the time, the Mazda developed idiosyncratic problems, so I traded it in on a Dodge van with a bed and mini kitchen. Soon I had two sons and the van was practical—I put an amazing 300,000 miles on it. It saw me through the nadir of my life, which turned around when I traded it in on a new '86 Maxima with "advanced electronics": an onboard "computer" that monitored average speed, miles per gallon and such. To read this Mickey-Mouse wonder, I had to duck my head down to see the screen near my right ankle, so it was also a hazard. It got me through a gut-wrenching divorce and was a pleasure till I ran out of money, again, and again met the repo man—after my friend Walt Bowart's pretty young trophy wife took the Maxima for a spin off road and wrecked the undercarriage. Back in the early sixties, Walt had launched what was then called "the underground press" with the *East Village Other* weekly newspaper. Walt also had written *Mind Control*, a book that was confiscated by the CIA "protecting freedom and democracy in America." When we reconnected twenty years later, Walt was editor of the *Palm Springs Magazine* and feeling disheartened by the new corporate imperative: Infomercials.

During my Maxima phase, I hooked up with my present wife Carolyn and our two grade-school-age sons liked to do "radio shows" from the Maxima's trunk, which opened into the backseat. They would imitate the car's recorded voice ("Right door is open") with announcements such as, "Stop at McDonalds," or "Go to money machine." Carolyn and I were pulling ourselves up from practically homeless to middle class with a house in the suburbs. During the past two decades we owned (and/or made payments on) an old Toyota Cressida that ran like a Swiss watch, then a little Toyota Celica that collided with a heat-buckled road surface and went airborne, wrecking its undercarriage. By 2000 we decided we needed only one car so traded those two in on the Acura RL, three years old when we bought it for about the price of a new Chevy.

Did someone say, "Spiking gas prices"?

When OPEC decided to punish Americans for siding with Israel in the 1970s, there was a gas shortage. During the first decade of the 21st Century there was—and as I write this still is—a gas price spike engineered by the big oil executives, who are now part of the corporate elite who virtually owns and operates our federal government and media. The corptocracy and their lobbyists write our laws and guide our thinking with their version of the news, saving us from the hot debates of democracy.

"These gas prices are thievery!"

"What are you gonna do? You can't fight city hall."

Seems only yesterday I was covering elections in Western Pennsylvania in my old Porsche, watching long lines of babushka-clad women from Eastern European Soviet Bloc countries, dutifully vote. Most didn't speak English or read, so they were aided by "poll watchers," who guided their hands to the candidate of the union's choice, where they penciled an X. By the time the second and third generation of this wave of immigrants became adults, the steel companies had moved overseas to escape paying American wages, leaving mill towns looking war-ravaged.

Where we now vote in Rehoboth Beach, Delaware, our polling place parking lot is full of high-tech cars which cost more than a house cost fifty years ago, and the new computerized voting machines require only that you finger-tip touch the name of the candidate of your choice. Turns out many of these wondrous machines were programmed to tally up a Republican win. Well, a lot of money is at stake. The war in Iraq costs about $2 billion a week, most of it pocketed by major shareholders in the military-industrial complex. George Bush is definitely the best president those folks ever had. He transfers money from the bankers of the Fed to his best campaign contributors, and sticks taxpayers with the bill at ever-compounding interest. God bless America. Have our intrepid leaders thought through the long-range consequences? Or does it matter? In the long run, as economist John Maynard Keynes said, we're all dead. If stupid greed doesn't end our American experiment, global warming appears ready to do the job.

With this dour thought in mind, in the spring of 2007 I drove the Acura a couple hundred miles north to attend a reunion of my high school graduating class. Feeling like a failure in my chosen career, I'd been reluctant to attend. But curiosity about my old schoolmates got me there.

We grew up in what was legally described as "a home and school for poor, white, male, fatherless orphans." We were born into the Great Depression before the USA had Social Security. Some of us didn't yet know English when, as six and seven year olds, we entered Girard College (the French word for school). Back in the 1930s Girard was so well endowed, it cherry-picked teachers from Andover, Exeter and other expensive prep schools. It was a kind of social experiment. Take some kids from the dregs of society, provide them with an expensive preppy type education and see what happens. My father had been killed in an auto accident when I was 11 months old. If he'd lived he would have become a brain surgeon. My mother, widowed with a baby on the cusp of the Great Depression, had been traumatized.

At this banquet in the Philadelphia suburbs, I hear the names of childhood friends coming from the mouths of old geezers I could pass on the street without recognizing. I'd lived most of my life in California and hadn't seen these guys in 50 years. But I recognize the voice of my teammate Jack Gerrighty when he singsongs, "Hey-eh-eh-eh Bobby!" like it was only yesterday. Our swim team won the Eastern States High School Championship. I learn that Jack got a BA before he wound up in the Marines. Then, instead of sending him to Korea, the Marines assigned him to lifeguard duty.

Jack and I are the only ones here from our championship team. I'm surprised to learn that Eddie Verdeur, our star freestyler, is dead, and that he had a brief major league baseball career. We recall our coach's daily search for his car. Coach Donlevy could never seem to remember where he'd parked, so after practice the team fanned out in search of his car. Indoor swimming season occurs in the middle of winter, so hither and yon we went through the coldest, bleakest weather of the year. Upon locating the car, one of us relayed the news on legs rubbery from a hard swimming workout.

Coach Donlevy was peculiar in other ways too. He believed in "land training" when most swimming coaches considered it absurd or harmful, and he believed in classical music. He'd get his swim team running around the track, doing push-ups and chin-ups, then bring us into the natatorium reverberating with the sounds of "The Beautiful Blue Danube" at full volume. We'd grouse about it and try to get him to play jitterbug music but he believed the classics helped our development.

After graduating from high school and being discharged from Girard, most of us floundered for a time, as institutional life does not prepare one for normal society. Those who survived Korea availed themselves of the GI Bill and got university degrees. A few of us got athletic scholarships and one got through Harvard on an academic scholarship. A few struggled up corporate ladders from mailrooms to boardrooms. A few committed suicide. Girard had indoctrinated us to be high achievers, but for many of us, graduation was like being released from prison without the benefit of a halfway house.

After the banquet, while driving to a motel with Jack's greeting ringing in my ear, I ponder what's new. Will global warming make human habitation of Planet Earth impossible? Or, having graduated from swooping seas under full sails to swooping interstates under full oil-gushing throttle, might we soon be swooping the heavens in Buck Rogers suits powered by the inexhaustible energy of earth's gravity? Maybe one of the African American kids now growing up in Girard, which has become almost 100 percent minority and coed, will figure out how.

Albert Goldbarth

You Might Notice Blood in Your Urine for a Couple of Weeks/Scenes from the American Revolution

I was like a taster that the kings use;
if the grapes are fatal, the taster dies.
And so all of my male friends my age
were almost as anxious waiting
for the report on my prostate biopsy
as I was. I was their crystal ball,
their tea leaves. I was the lure for an unguessable catch.
"What is it like?" (Not that they ever asked this
so forthrightly.) How does it feel, in the fogs and
      cumulonimbus
of the land of indeterminacy?
And my answer included fear of course but more than that,
a greed for even the beauty of the scantest bead
of spray-on damp
bejeweling the florets of broccoli at the salad bar
as they refuse to wilt, for even a single lash
that fringed my wife's shut eye and fed in her sleep
on its own minute allotment of oils. . . I wouldn't yield
any portion of these to oblivion, nothing
too subepidermal or superlunary

for my newfound and possibly short-lived care,
and when these friends of mine were going hormonally gaga
over a stripper's slinky, fleshy pleats and impeccable smoothness,
I could have wept for staring at *nothing*
more articulate and lovely than the way
the shadows under her breasts reminded me of the vowels
under Hebrew and Arabic consonants — I wouldn't overlook
     a single
calorie of exuded human warmth. One night I bit a book
to see my teethmarks, to remind me I had saliva and will,
and out of a taste for the paper itself. The book was *Patriots*
(A. J. Langguth). In chapter 17, a troop of colonial soldiers
     suffers the frozen swamps and brambled forests of the
march up to Quebec.
They lose their rations. They boil their moccasins for soup.
When those are gone, they wrap their bleeding feet in flour bags
and continue. They can't *not* continue on, or hug the last
bedraggled, shitty, wonderful shred of themselves to themselves.
They kill the captain's great black slobbery dog
and eat everything including its guts, then gather the bones
and pound them to dust and brew a greenish broth of that.
They dole this out like a fine Madeira wine
and smack their lips and swirl their tongues.
Because they won't let go.
Because they still have lips and tongues.

●

A woman is darning a petticoat.
Outside her window it's April 18, 1775,
And the very air tonight is heavier
and charged, as if the revolution announces its close approach
the way a storm would . . . so the boughs of trees seem dense

with whispering thought like rows of brains, and the dirt
stirs out of its ease in ways that alarm the chickens from sleep.
Buckshot is being stored up; swanshot; grapeshot.
This is the night that Paul Revere sets down
that client's teeth he's carving out of a diced-down hippopotamus
    tusk;
his mission is to row across the Charles, undetected
by a hulking British man-of-war, the *Somerset*,
and deliver a warning to Hancock and Adams in Lexington.
Empire! Liberty! Carnage! — huge ideas encumber the night.
But we can't fault this woman for smaller attention,
to her garment and its rip. Her frugal life.
Her dainty fingers that we can imagine just as readily
stroking a lover's hair, some young man done for the day
at the barrel-maker's and hurrying up her stairs
for the pleasureful rumpus that momentarily outweighs
even a memory of the bundles of staves on his shoulders.
As she stitches, she's naked: a breeze is an intimate
touch she's always appreciated. And when she's finished
mending it, she slips back into the petticoat: the air by now
is too cool, and she draws the curtain shut, and sits here,
quietly enjoying the heat of her body as it doubles back
upon itself, deliciously, under her ruffles. I would like to think
that this is an implicit understanding of how all too soon
all flesh is too, too cool: and any tiniest resistance is a victory
against that. By the morning, Deacon Hayes would be dead,
killed by a British shot as he reloaded his musket.
And old Jonas Parker: dead. And a wounded British soldier
—his head was split to the brain-meat by a Massachusetts boy
who came upon him with a tomahawk. Altogether,
forty-nine American bodies cooling in the dawn sun, and
(the long guns used to hunt duck proved effective) seventy-three
of the British infantrymen. What *would* I say

if my long week of impatiently waiting a lab report were spent
back there, in gathering intelligence for communiqués
snuck forward to the future? I don't know; although
I'm picturing my friends around the amber glow
of a pitcher of beer in bar light, when it suddenly
and mysteriously pours sound forth, like a radio,
and a gargle of homilies interrupts their boozy talk:
Love every stitch. Remember every thread. And so they startle;
then shrug; and go on joking. In any case, I'm not there.
Paul Revere is there. In his worry and haste,
he's neglected to bring the cloths that he normally uses
to muffle the plash of his oars. But luckily,
one of the young men who'd been appointed to accompany him
on this clandestine launch—a slim, wisecracking
barrel-maker's assistant—leads them to his sweetheart's house
and whistles below her window. When she learns the problem,
she removes her petticoat and flings it, as she might a kiss,
to the deepening chill of the night air. A. J. Langguth:
"The flannel was still warm when it was passed to Paul Revere."

126

photo by
Minna Proctor

Walter Cummins

After Aging

What comes after aging? Most likely the finality of the Monty Python dead parrot sketch: 'E's kicked the bucket, 'e's shuffled off 'is mortal coil, rung down the curtain and joined the bleedin' choir invisible!! This Is An Ex-Aging Male!

Considering that alternative, getting old isn't so bad. But it's out there—the inevitable farm waiting to be bought. One of the existentialists—Martin Heidegger, I believe—said something to the effect that a person really doesn't get in touch with his existence until he fully understands that it's not enough to say, "One dies," but that it must be "I will die."

Sure. But me? I know many people who have died, been close to a number and actually been present at the moment of death. Still, I get up every morning, drink a cup of coffee, read the headlines and the comics, clean the litter box, check my email, and perform the rest of my daily rituals as if I'll be doing them forever. A somewhat rational being, I know it can't go on indefinitely. I can't go on. But Heidegger would be disappointed in me. I don't live with the overriding consciousness of my non-being. Yet I think about it from time to time.

Obituaries

When reading the morning paper, somewhere between the

Mets box score and the editorial page, I scan the obituaries to see if anyone I know or know of has left us, an occasion to shake my head and tell my wife, "Guess who died?" And I also check the ages of the deceased.

On one recent day among the four full pages of obits, sixty-two names, I mentally sorted the dead into three categories. Donna was 44, John 47, Todd 55, poor Calvin only 17, even sadder, Joseph only two and a half. These and others make up the group younger than I, those I have the perverse satisfaction of having outlived. Benedict was 95, Marie 88, Carmine 86, Joe 94, Florence 93. This group gives me a certain amount of comfort, the possible expectation of years ahead. If Benedict and Florence can do it, why not me?

What brings me up short are all those in my age range. Doris 74, Vincent 73, Audrey 73, Martin 65, Elizabeth 68. There I'd be — Walter 75, my ended life summed up in five or six column inches, a handful of people shaking heads and tapping the arm of a partner, "Guess who died?" Then the paper discarded for recycling.

Photos

Our northern New Jersey daily often prints photos with obits, pictures provided by the family, the subject usually smiling at an age years younger than that at which he or she passed on. It must be the way loved ones want to remember them, not gaunt and gasping as they were on their deathbeds.

That's usually the way it is with other people—friends from the past, acquaintances, celebrities. The image in our memories is fixed in time, how they looked once, at their prime. For us their identities are static, and we're often shocked to see them different— the classmate you last saw when he was twenty now an elderly man. But in our relationships with ourselves we're always in process; our state at the moment is what matters most, our understanding of who we are, the past like a novel we once read, most of it far less vivid than the book on our nightstand.

In my wallet I carry a university ID with a picture taken around twenty-five years ago. On the rare occasions I've looked at it in the past, I've thought to myself that I hadn't changed all that much. My glasses are different, tinted aviators long out of style now. But recently I decided to compare that photo with the very recent mug shot on my credit card. That certainly turned out to be a reality check. No doubt about it. I've been transformed into an archetypal aging male.

Funerals

Over the years I've attended many funerals and memorial services and on occasions joined the cavalcade to the cemetery for interment. Funerals tend to follow a pattern, people entering the church or hall or tabernacle in nervous, hushed silence, making quick eye contact with others they know, then sitting with folded hands as they wait for the service to begin, occasionally whispering to the person next to them. The coffin rests at the front of the assemblage, often surrounded by wreaths and flower arrangements and a photo of the deceased in happier days. All the time mournful music sounds in the background. Finally, the priest-minister-rabbi enters and the service begins. Prayers, hymns, eulogy. Usually, at least in my experience, friends and relations get up to say something, the designated adult offspring choked and nervous, fighting back tears, next someone not as close voicing regrets and telling anecdotes about the deceased, eliciting smiles and then laughter, everyone relieved now, at ease with the occasion. Death isn't so bad. He/she had a good life. Remember the time …

After the last hymn and the final prayers, everyone stands to line up for handshakes and embraces with the surviving family members. Kisses on cheeks, hands touched, pats on backs. Then people mingle, glad to see old friends, smiling openly at each other now, sharing memories of the dead one and asking about people who aren't in attendance. Sons, daughters, parents, siblings. It turns into a social occasion, an excuse for some to have traveled miles, plans made for dinner, promises to get together soon. Hugs and happiness.

The corpse in the box shrinks to the back of everyone's attention, the coffin already a familiar object in the room, something the eye passes over that barely registers. For all but a few the dead one is already history, a memory of someone they knew once, not nearly as interesting as the breathing beings around them, people who have a future in their lives. And why not? We've got to move on, have a drink, eat a sandwich, stop at the supermarket on our way home to catch the end of the ball game.

Depending on the denomination, during the service the clergy person may speak of the life to come, redemption and bliss. Evoking the afterlife.

Afterlife

Unlike the majority of Americans, according to opinion surveys, I have no expectation of any form of existence to follow this one, adhering to the philosophy of the old beer commercial— you only go around once, so grab all the gusto you can. (I've often wondered why the millions who oppose stem cell research never rose up in mass protest over the blasphemy of that slogan, or at a minimum urged a boycott of the beer.)

Sure, it would be nice to see my parents and my brother and sisters, and Mookie, my cat of sixteen years, and Rex, my dog of childhood. But for all eternity, time everlasting? We'd run out of things to say to each other, get sick of repeating the same memories of life on earth over and over. I can envision us muttering under our breaths, "Get a life," oblivious to the irony of that impossibility. Even Rex would tire of pats on the head, Mookie of rubs under his chin. They might even, after a century or two, snarl and snap. And I wouldn't blame them.

Here's an unrhymed terza rima from Longfellow's translation of Dante's Paradise:

> O grace abundant, by which I presumed
> To fix my sight upon the Light Eternal,
> So that the seeing I consumed therein!

It has some appeal, I suppose. Instead of Mom and Pop, cat and dog, I'd ascend to a vision of Light Eternal. But then what? Wouldn't it pale after a millennium or two?

Gym

I work out, try to make it a priority to spend time at the gym at least three days a week, a ritual I started about ten years ago. Most of my life I'd never been one for systematic exercise, probably a reaction to my uncoordinated youth, when if I did get into a pickup baseball game, I'd end up in right field with a fifty-fifty chance of catching the rare fly balls that came in my direction. Yet there came a time when men my age were advised to keep in shape.

My start was tentative, just time on a treadmill, a bit embarrassed to be in the midst of all those student athletes decades younger, women with cute tattoos on the small of their backs who could run for hours on the treadmill next to mine, bulky guys whose thick biceps bore images of chain links and elaborate crosses hoisting weighted barbells high over their heads. Me wondering what would happen if I raised the pace on my machine above four miles an hour.

Now I'm on the elliptical trainer, tugging on the weight machines, pushing back on the head and neck extender, no longer thinking that this is no country for old men, no longer wondering if the young, taking a break from being in each others arms, consider me a paltry thing, a tattered coat upon a stick.

Some days, especially during summer break, most of the men

in the gym are geezers like me, a couple looking as if they were retired drill sergeants, bald heads tanned and gleaming. On such days old men have taken over the country, pumping and stepping and lifting in their defiance of mortality.

Diet

I'm fortunate to have a wife with long experience as a medical writer who is nutritionally informed and wants to keep me around. Over the time of our marriage, she's informed and reformed me. We eat healthy, with zero tolerance for transfats, minimizing saturated fats, opting for whole grains, yogurt, fresh salads, green vegetables, fruits and nuts. Salt and mayonnaise are anathema to me.

I take vitamins and supplements too, every morning like clockwork—a multiple, calcium with more D, 81 mg aspirin, Beta-sitosterol, omega 3, glucosamine chondroitin. I'm working at it to keep my joints lubricated, my bones firm, my triglycerides in check, my circulation wooshing along.

Blood

But like my late parents and siblings, I have a tendency toward high blood pressure, mine medicated as soon as it reached 140 over 90. After various combinations my doc settled on HCT (the standard diuretic that keeps me going and going day and night) and a generic Ace inhibitor. They work, keep my pressure artificially normal.

Feeling the call to some version of public service, I started donating blood several decades ago. That's how I realized my blood pressure was rising, when the nurse checked me. The first couple of times I assumed it was an aberration, then saw the doctor, who checked me sitting up and lying down and fifteen minutes later, I'd reached a stage in life where I needed pills. Even medicated I was still able to donate.

That is, until I fainted. Not at the blood center but that evening after a potluck dinner with a group of friends. The blood center had called lamenting severe shortages, people in need, even for my mundane O positive, I considered the donation an excuse to eat a Twinkie, a concoction of sugary pulp I don't even like. Drink plenty of fluids, the nurse advised. Avoid alcohol for two hours

My intention was to drive home and relax with chilled glasses of flavored seltzer. But a half-mile from the blood center, the Check Engine warning flashed, followed by a message about a brake light problem. I ended up spending the afternoon sitting in the dealer's service area listening to the inane cell phone conversations of the woman next to me. That should have been a clue that this wasn't going to be my day.

After several hours of conversation and sampling the food, including a glass of white wine now that far more than two hours had passed, I was standing at a kitchen island listening to a man explain the talks he gave at mathematical conferences, when I realized I couldn't think of a single intelligent comment to make. Not that I'd have much to say about advanced math in the best of circumstances. But this felt odd, my mind bogged down in mental sludge. Within seconds I was drenched in a cold, clammy sweat, suddenly nauseous.

When I opened my eyes, I found myself sitting cross-legged on the floor, a young woman I had never seen before taking my pulse. She was, I soon learned, the daughter of a guest, an emergency medical technician who lived two houses down and had gotten there in a flash during the time I had been unconscious. About a minute according to those hovering over me. "I'm going to throw up," I announced, someone handed me a plastic pan, and I did. My wife began applying wet paper towels to my forehead, and cold water ran down my shirtfront.

"I think we should call the rescue squad," the EMT daughter told the huddled group. They nodded, seconding the motion. So, despite my protesting that it was just my lack of fluids, I ended up in the hospital for several days, my heart continuously monitored, my carotid arteries checked with a Doppler test, my ticker evaluated with an echocardiogram.

I was fine, released after great expense to Medicare. But my doc told me to stop donating blood, assuring me that I had given my share, and, besides, I was a man my age.

Hospital

Every time I visit someone in the hospital and see the friend or relative stretched under a white sheet, a plastic ID looped around a wrist, needles in each arm, drip bags suspended behind them, machines blipping, I get the sense of otherness. The person has been transformed into an object to be poked and tested and wheeled about by medical professionals. Strangers do to and for you. Volition is gone and with it the dignity of being a functioning person. And after each visit I wonder how I would feel when I became the patient.

Until my fainting, I hadn't been in the hospital for decades. At ten I had pneumonia, at sixteen an ear infection, conditions that would be treated at home with drugs these days. In my thirties I spent a couple of days in for tests. Now here I was delivered by the local rescue squad, lifted from gurney to bed, all the time thinking, this is a mistake. I don't belong here. I want to go home.

In fact, I was only a few days from a flight to Europe, felt compelled to give that information to anyone who tended to me — doctors, nurses, technicians, the woman who delivered meals. Even though I had to wear a gown, I kept my pants on, my socks too, poised for a quick getaway. Fortunately, the last nurse assigned to me had just returned from a trip to the Amalfi coast. We chatted about places and she sympathized, got me released right after the echocardiogram results cleared me.

Of course, it's quite likely that I'll be a real patient someday, too sick to resist, the nurses grim, my doctor asking if I had prepared a living will.

Nursing Home

That prospect is even scarier than the hospital. I've visited in bad ones and good ones. In the bad, the residents were lined up in wheelchairs outside their rooms, eyes closed, chins on their chests as if they were drugged, and probably were. The place smelled of disinfectant and urine. In the good—good in the sense that it cost a great deal, didn't smell, and had a location in a very affluent town—when you walked down the hall, you saw many of the residents comatose in their beds, white hair wispy, pale flesh brittle, jaws dropped. Those awake were aligned in front of blaring TV sets gaping at programs so far removed from the states of their existences that they could have been beamed from Mars. Or they might be in a day room where chipper entertainers were trying to lead group sings of turns like "I'm Looking Over a Four-leaf Clover," all sound coming from the people at the piano, a few other mouths barely moving.

In my limited experience, by far most of the residents were women. Aging males may be kicking off before they reach that state. Lucky them.

Symptoms

With my blood pressure under control, my doc tells me I'm in good shape for a man my age. How long can that last? Every once in a while I get a pain in my gut or a tightening in my chest. I've had them before, and they've always gone away. A bug in my system, heartburn, gas. But someday I'll have a pain, a throb, a clutching that will be for real. It may be a harbinger of a long decline or a sign of sudden termination. Like all aging men, I will die.

The Moving Finger

In these modern days we have to update Omar Khayyam and say "the aging finger types." Still, having writ, it "Moves on: nor all your Piety nor Wit / Shall lure it back to cancel half a Line, / Nor all your Tears wash out a Word of it." I have a fantasy about moving aging fingers on my own death bed, propped up with an elevated mattress, a mini computer in my hand or maybe a cell phone for text messaging, and me able to articulate and record all the sensations of my death throes, down to the last instant, entering the very last period of my writing career just as breath stops and rigor begins. "That's all she [in this case, he] wrote." The device pried from my cold, dead, ex-aging male hand.

James Campbell
Kick Bucket

Jack Marshall

Sickbed Redux

Sickbed's a better place
Than many to review your state
Of health, or lack thereof…space-
Yawning window looking out

On a receding world far
Wider than its width, as swift
Stimuli on the surface—air,
Light, speech, touch—drift

Out of reach, to the bottom
Of thought, to thought
With a clarity seen from
Below, where you're caught

Aging face in a mirror
Silvered with years is covering
A child's heart. A mirror
Holds many faces, but no heart. Hovering

Shadow released from earthly weight,
Blankness, too, is part of the bargain,
As is the autumn-aching note

Of Brahms' last clarinet solo. What's broken
Spits curses in disillusion, kissed
So deep it can't be shrugged off.
Now all your noble vows must
Vie with their larval undertow and the rough

Bitterness the mortally ill feel
Entitled to, when the ways we've thought
Predicate unpredictable
Ploys ignite a fate

Unimaginable, far off, still to come,
Making the most of rust; envying
The mayfly's life spun
Of a half day of minutes; whirling

Like a bird faced with the end
Of flying. At the end, everything becomes
Clear, but unchangeable, and as we tend
Downward, toward what we cannot name,

In an unrest held fast, or
A touch, neither reassuring nor mild,
God doesn't care
Whether what grows is a child

Or cancer, or if we can know
How mindless, measureless,
Long, wide, and deep now
May reach the speechless vocalese of bliss,

Or if, as with knife and fork, we lift
A rainbow from a salmon's scales,
Or travel out toward the reddest shift,
Or, ebbing grace-note, end in gravel.

Greg Herriges

My Kid Brother

I wake as a reaction to nothing, perhaps just the June sunlight that has insinuated itself beneath the slats of the vertical blinds of the bedroom, or else to the insistent barking of a dog down the block, the harrumph of a car door slamming below. It's not like it was in the old days, when the clock radio would jolt me out of sleep with a.m. radio static, followed by an asinine commercial jingle, or a really bad news headline: *Your Antiperspirant Could Be Killing You.* Dutifully, I would throw on a pair of jeans, go downstairs to make a pot of coffee, and lock myself in a little room to write for the next three hours, inspired or otherwise. Often otherwise. That was when I was young and I had what passed for discipline. It was my own little secret that what I really had was just a case of obsessive-compulsive disorder. I've now outgrown even that.

I can go six months at a time without writing a damned thing. That's progress.

But the coffee remains a constant. I shuffle off to the kitchen to make a cup of instant. I haven't the patience anymore to wait for a whole pot of the stuff to drip through a gauze-like filter, drain down a ridiculously tiny aperture, nor do I have the need for caffeine in such quantity. I open the blinds in the living room and gaze out at the thicket of brush and trees just beyond the edge of the lawn, at birds in frenzied, zigzag flight—white-breasted nuthatches, purple martins, dark-eyed juncos. At times I have come face-to-face with deer, or else I've spied foxes, wild rabbits. This is our vacation home in the Wisconsin woods, the only place on earth I can find some genuine, durable peace. I have senesced my way to the top of the seniority list at the college, though I am still needed there four days a week. The rest of the time I am here, reading, hiking. Sometimes I even forget that I am old.

But the truth will not be ignored. It nudges its way forward, importunes, shouts down my illusions. It does this by way of three degenerated discs that stab at my spinal cord the way hungry seafood diners attempt to pry Maine lobster out of the shell. Once the pain was so bad for such a prolonged period that a specialist gave me morphine lollipops, while a neurosurgeon advised me to have cadaver bone inserted in my spinal column and held in place with a titanium screw. He said he would make the incision in my throat and move my voice box over while he drilled from the front of my body at the discs.

"But couldn't that damage my voice?" I asked him.

He narrowed his eyelids to paper-thin slits, gave me a suspicious, interrogatory, medical look. "What are you," he asked, "an *opera* singer?"

I know how old I am. I'm almost as old as my father was when he died. This is good and bad. He died young, so I'm not as old as I *could* be. But I lose words. Especially in the middle of a lecture at the college in my writing classes, I lose words. I smile. I study the tips of my shoes for clues. I tell my students, "Oops, the software is down again." Sometimes they laugh and think I'm kidding, but by the end of the semester they know I am not, and they believe me.

But today is one of those days that serves as a reprieve. For some reason, a reason that remains a pleasant mystery to me, I feel really good today, spry, chipper. Who wouldn't want another chance? You don't look a gift horse in his orifice, and so I sip my coffee leisurely, bask under the hot therapeutic spray of the shower, and watch my wife as she combs her long hair, counting my blessings along the way. My son for instance, all grown up, recently graduated from college, and professionally employed, no less. He's back home, probably sleeping late, or else watching a sporting event on TV, beside him a novel face-down on the couch (the same couch upon which we used to wrestle each other when he was six). He's a high school English teacher now. He lifts weights. He writes stories and screenplays. He's a miracle and has been well cared for.

The car top is down. My wife and I cruise route 50, wending our way over rolling green hills, between expansive fields of tall corn and open horse corrals, golden sunshine spread in sheets before us, behind us; it's everywhere. I think, *And when my son and I used to wrestle, I was amazed at the strength of the boy, delighted by his shrieks of joy, and of course I always let him win at the last minute.*

My cell phone rings. It plays the opening lines of "Just Like Starting Over," a song I have to identify to most people, because it has been thirty-one years since it was number one on *Billboard*'s Hot 100 List.

"Hello?"

Coincidentally, synchronously, as if he knew I was thinking of him, it is my son, and from here onward the narrative trail grows dark, takes ominous twists, propels me in directions I do not want to go. But I haven't any choice. My brother is dying.

•

We grew up in the Kodak-blue, suburban 1950s, the sons of a Midwestern banker and his wife. I was older by two years. It was easy back then to find your way around in the world. There were Fords and Chevies and Dinah Shore and Jackie Gleason and the Ravinia Music Festival, which my parents used to listen to from our back yard, sitting in their aluminum patio chairs under north shore stars. They would let us know who was playing or singing. "That's Duke Ellington," my father would say. My brother and I were catching lightning bugs in a jar. We thought Duke Ellington might be visiting royalty. Lee, my kid brother, discovered that if you crushed the bugs, their luminescence would spread across the sidewalk and light up a patch of concrete.

I rode a 26-inch J.C. Higgins bicycle from the Sears catalogue. It was all red and chrome and had two built-in lights that rusted overnight and quit working. Lee had a 24- inch Raleigh, and though it was smaller, it was actually a more finely engineered machine when it came to handling curves and making tight turns. Truth be known, and I tried to suppress this truth for as long as I could, Lee learned to ride a good year before I could. I'd had a bad run-in with a brick wall of a supermarket while trying to learn balance. I spent the afternoons of the greater part of six months inside dental clinics trying to save my second teeth. Lee was pretty good about not rubbing it in—my unspeakable failure as a big brother. I was supposed to be teaching him how to ride.

I'm the one who left his Raleigh bike in the driveway the day Mom backed the red Ford station wagon over it, turning it into a pretzel-cycle. I don't think I jumped up immediately to claim the blame.

Dad took Lee and me camping one weekend up at Apple River Canyon near Galena, Illinois. We fished lazily in the dappled sunlight under the huge, gnarled limbs of canyon trees, our bobbers gently riding the waters of the river, while I turned the pages of a Superboy comic book, learning about the whimsically unpredictable qualities of red Kryptonite. It could make you lose your memory or give you a twin, if you were from Krypton. Suddenly, as if taunting me in my moment of serenity, my bobber tore loose from my line, and I had to endure the humiliation of running downstream over slippery rocks in a vain attempt to retrieve it. We never caught any fish on that trip. How could we, with me jumping in the stream, announcing our presence, scaring the fish away?

I do remember, though, having a bad dream that evening,

under the big quilt in our tent. I woke up shivering in fear and in reaction to the chill of the Apple River Canyon night to tell Lee about the German soldiers I'd seen ready to attack us behind the ridge of trees. "It was a dream, I think," I told him, although I was still not entirely convinced of this myself. German soldiers were a real concern in those days, the subject of many a movie, and new TV dramas like "Combat!" I remember Lee staying awake after that, carefully eyeing the inky shadows of the foliage silently moving in the breeze. One couldn't be too careful in the dark, so far from home, the enemy troops and their machine gun nests hiding, invisible in the Midwestern night, along the Illinois-Berlin border.

•

My wife and I take our seats in the back of an American Airlines jetliner, hoping that the third person of the row will treat us kindly by staying home. We are headed for Orlando, Florida. My brother is on a ventilator in a hospital near Kissimmee, a hospital almost ghoulishly named *Celebration Hospital*. When my son called on the cell phone while we were in the sheets of sunshine in Wisconsin, it was with the news that our local police dispatcher had phoned him. A woman (let's call her Julia) had called them to say she wanted to get in touch with us, that my brother was gravely ill with a lung disorder. She didn't know our phone number—it is unlisted, and the police are not allowed to give out that information. They can, however, deliver messages, on easy summer days when sons are asleep, when parents are cruising down route 50 toward Kenosha, not a care in the world.

The pilot turns on the seatbelt lights as we get ready to taxi. There are all those mysterious noises down below in the cargo area, doors slamming shut, electric motors whirring, sounding vaguely like winches grinding. I recall speaking to Julia. She told me my

145

brother had changed his name, changed it legally to Mark Donavan. He had been working at an amusement park, living in a motel with a dog named Midnight. He'd been sick with bronchitis for quite a while, but refused medical treatment. Lee was always afraid of doctors and hospitals. *Mark* was, that is. I had not seen him in twenty-three years, since my wedding. No one in the family had seen him. He had disappeared, more or less. More.

The plane lurches forward and turns. My wife cups her hand over mine. She is a nurse. She has a pretty good idea what awaits us in Florida. I don't. I'm not in the medical loop. I don't care for doctors much more than Lee does. Than Mark does. And why did he have to change his name? How can someone wake up one morning and decide that he is someone else? I know there have been days when I have *wished* that I were someone else. Maybe that's what happened to Lee. Maybe he wished he were someone else so bad that one morning he wished himself right into being Mark Donavan.

•

Our grammar school back in 1960 was The Ravinia School. It was a large, red brick building that had been spliced together over the decades with several additions as the child population had expanded in that affluent suburb. There were twists and turns in the cavernous corridors, and several secret passageways (limned with Robin Hood murals) that only the most expert hallway roamer knew about. Our home was set about a mile away, and when Lee was a new student, it was my chore to pick him up at his classroom after school and walk him home. He was kind of a runt at that age, and I was the older brother, who guided him across busy streets and over the dreaded railroad tracks, upon which a woman and her little baby had been killed not so long ago, smashed in their automobile, which had come, for some reason, to a standstill on the tracks. The adults always referred to that incident in whispers to one another, behind the backs of their hands, as if that didn't make it irresistible for any children within hearing distance to listen all the harder. Of course we all knew about it too, and I can't speak for the others, but I always thought about them, especially the baby, whenever I crossed those ominous, silver-blue tracks. A squashed baby is not something that you forget.

And so it happened that one afternoon I had much on my mind after school, or else it was so glorious outside after having been pent up all day, that I forgot to stop by Lee's classroom to fetch him. Clean forgot. I didn't realize my stupendous mistake until I got to the railroad tracks upon which the baby, etc., and by the time I arrived breathless at the entrance of my brother's schoolroom, he was in the company of his teacher and mine, crying so horribly you would have thought a train had just missed him, or perhaps not missed him at all.

I kept trying to calm him down by telling him that it was all right, but he howled, and his face was red and slippery with desperate tears. My third grade teacher did not hesitate to share her true opinion of me, either. The words *irresponsible* and *thoughtless* spewed into the already chaotic scene, and I wondered if the frazzled, wobbly world would ever get back to its old, calm self. Not soon, it didn't. The whole scene was repeated with my mother once we got back home and my name was mud for at least a week. It was around this time that I decided the Raleigh bike incident might as well remain a life-long secret.

•

The thick air of the Florida summer night greets us as we enter Orlando's Peabody Hotel. "Jesus," I say, alarmed at the extravagance of the place. "What's this costing us?"

"It's a package deal," my wife says, code for *You'd better not*

147

ask. But it really is extraordinary, the size and splendor, the many sitting rooms with overstuffed couches, conference rooms, marble, polished brass. And ducks. Everywhere I look there are embossed ducks. I just want a quick drink and then our room, the comfort of a soft bed and a night's sleep.

I study the chill wonders of the scotch surrounding the melting glaciers of ice cubes in my glass. "So you're sure it's HIV?" I ask.

My wife nods. "The hospital staff can't come out and tell you because of the FEMA laws. But the blood count, the Kaposi's sarcoma, and the fact that they wanted someone to make the decision to take him off life support, all make it obvious."

We know this much. Mark had respiratory failure and had been on a ventilator for nine days. A hospital representative referred to the Kaposi's sarcoma, though not by name, just referred to it as skin lesions. I cannot alone accept power of attorney for Lee because we have two other siblings. Under Florida law, at least two siblings must accept that power of attorney together, and that is not going to happen, not in my family, not with my siblings. But we are here because he has regained consciousness, suddenly, unexpectedly. In the morning I will see my brother. I will be able to talk to him. I don't know that I will get any answers about his life, what has become of him, and I don't know that I want any. But we can talk.

Ducks, I think, tilting my glass, finishing the scotch. *Why all the ducks?*

The hospital is a beautiful place, new, well-maintained, judging by the impeccable state of the grounds, the buildings. I have a bag of gifts for my brother: a CD player with headphones, a collection of Ricky Nelson songs, The Beatles' *Revolver*, a copy of my new book. The ICU ward is on the third floor and a long walk away. I have plenty to think about.

•

"You don't take St. John's Avenue, and you don't take Greenbay Road, either," I excitedly told Lee. We were circling one another like sharks on wheels in a parking lot on Roger Williams Avenue in Ravinia. He'd gotten a new white 20 incher to replace the Raleigh. My fabulous discovery—a short cut to downtown Highland Park, only a five minute trip. We were the Lewis and Clark of bike routes—only this one must have had a black hole connected to it. I showed him one late afternoon, and sure enough, bingo. Grant & Grant Record Store was now a few heartbeats from our back yard. I didn't know how this was possible. I still don't. But we rode there together, and barely having worked up a sweat, we parked our bikes, and pooled our loose change. Together we had enough for two 45 RPM records. Mine was an easy choice—Dion's "Love Came To Me." I liked that deep-Bronx New York rock. Lee had more mainstream musical tastes, LA-residential. He went with Ricky Nelson's "Young World," a worthy song, in my estimation. On the way home I discovered that if you removed a handlebar grip, you could slide the 45 disc onto the smooth chrome surface of the handlebar itself, and then seal it in by replacing the grip. Quite an innovation.

When you're in love, you're in a young world
I think he played that song for a month straight.

●

"Can we just go in?" I say.

The nurse is a good-natured young woman with a caramel complexion and pretty white teeth. "Yes, he won't be able to speak to you, though. His throat has been damaged."

She sees that I need the moral support, I suspect, and so she accompanies us into the room. "Mark, look. I've brought you guests—your brother and his wife."

He is alone in the room, in his life, in the universe. His

149

solitude is nearly palpable, a man used to living by himself, a boy. He has shrunken away into nothing. Sixty-five pounds, they say, his emaciated skull atop a reed-like neck that cannot even support it, no, not even in a reclining position. I swallow. I go into high gear to conceal my astonishment.

"Hey, pal. Nice to see you once every century. You could've at least called, for Christ's sake."

My wife moves right up to him, puts her hand on his bare arm, caresses his full head of hair. His mouth and nose are covered by a transparent breathing cup attached to an oxygen hose. He stares unflinchingly—long glances, as if he is trying to soak us up with his eyes. What comes across immediately is his inability to do anything for himself. His head literally slides down his pillow to his shoulder. I ease my way between IV stands and plastic hoses to move his head back into place. It falls down again. There are no stabilizing muscles. I have to hold his head firmly between my hands, keep it there, while his eyes roll, dizzily. From time to time they will dart and light upon some object in the room, a chair, a bed stand, my face. Then his lids slowly close and reopen and he looks deep into my eyes, as if trying to project a thought, to reach me with some wild, secret information. I don't know what it is he is trying to say. When he senses his failure to communicate, he gives up the effort, shifts his gaze to the ceiling, to the wall. He looks utterly drained and without hope.

We dance this dance several times, and it occurs to me in a stomach-sinking flash that this is all there is left for us to do.

The young nurse saves the day. She bustles around the room and opens the blinds. "Mark, are you happy to see your brother?"

He blinks.

"Is he your older brother?" she asks, adjusting his bed position, re-stacking his pillows.

"Yes," I say for him.

"Did he used to beat you up?"

Lee's eyes . . . Mark's eyes, widen.

"I was merciless," I say, putting a light spin upon the truth. "Absolutely merciless, wasn't I, buddy?"

He blinks in mute agreement.

"Look what I brought you," I say, emptying the bag, enumerating the contents. The CD player, batteries, a re-charger. "*Ricky Nelson's Greatest Hits*. When I went through Mom's record collection, I noticed you'd taken all of the old Ricky singles. Oh, and my new book."

He makes a funny face when I mention the book, a look of surprise, or pride. He isn't able to grasp it or hold it upright, and neither can he read it, but he is pleased, and so, for a moment, am I.

I am still regarding his hands, which rest on either side of him upon the bed, when Julia enters the room. I have never met Julia before, only spoken to her on the phone. She is some sort of law-enforcement officer, wears a uniform, and is slightly older than I imagined her.

She has good news about his dog, Midnight. She has taken him to the vet for his shots, and he is being well cared for. She has taken him in.

Funny, how much of a situation you don't understand when all you have is a voice on a phone. They are friends, she the nurturer, and once upon a time, I gather, she was more than that to him. Her presence has lightened the mood, and so too, everyone's immediate burden. Those hands at his sides, the ones that no longer work, are our father's hands. They look oddly husky on him, as though they could easily hold a plane, shave smooth the edges of a two-by-four. Above them, on his forearms, are open sores stretching all the way to his neck.

I was at first distracted because of the emotional gravity of this moment we have so awkwardly wandered into. But this is not another case of HIV. My brother is at the very last stages of full-blown AIDS. While the staff members have not directly confirmed this, they have alluded to it. His system is producing no blood cells. He has no immune system at all. What confounds me, sets this realization in deep relief against an otherwise familiar background of reality, is what the nurse says to me when I announce that we will be back later in the day: "He's doing so much better."

The original Peabody Hotel is in Memphis, and it was there in the 1930s that the tradition of putting ducks in the interior fountain began, and developed sometime later into a formal duck march. They actually play marching music and there is a Duckmaster with a brass, duck-head cane. My wife and I sit in the sunny atrium of the hotel listening to piano music, sipping wine. I feel distinctly guilty about the luxury of my respite between hospital visits. Mallard ducks swim in the frothy water of the fountain to the delight of guests who stop to bend over, gawk at them, talk to them. We are waiting on a visit from an old friend who graduated from Fort Lauderdale High School with me. My parents divorced while my brother and I were young, and one year when things at home became increasingly difficult, we followed my father to Florida and stayed there. At least, my brother stayed.

"He was always in trouble," I tell my wife, "since the nuns failed him in the fifth grade." Then I ask, before bringing my wine glass fully to my mouth, as though there still lingers a fair degree of disbelief and righteous indignation, "Why would anyone fail a fifth-grader?"

"They still failed children, back then," my wife answers.

But that is not what I mean. I'm looking for someplace to lay the carcass of blame for my brother's failures, which are many, the accruing trouble, some arrests. Nuns seem like a good place to start. I'd just as soon blame them as my parents, as life itself, for all the good blame will do.

It wasn't the nuns.

"He's not going to make it," I say, in the din of chatter and tinkling piano keys.

My wife says, "No, he's not."

I stand up, move against the current of guests, hoping for decent cell phone reception at the hotel entrance. In the glare of the Floridian sun I run smack into him, and for one slow second we share a greeting of mutual surprise at our good fortune, our unlikely good fortune.

"Keith." I pronounce his name as if it is corroboration. We shake hands. We embrace. He is older—there are taut lines in his face—but he is still tall and handsome, and there is a healthy light in his eyes. He carries with him optimism, as unselfconsciously as one can carry that good gift. I bring him to meet my wife in the glade of the atrium, and we have wine, and we laugh, twenty-nine years of shared absence melting in the midst of the piano music, sunlight, and ducks.

Keith and I met in Larry Stock's humanities class in 1967. We read Voltaire and Camus and Goethe and he knocked up his girlfriend and her father beat him bloody. They had a daughter and separated and he became a musician and a nutritional expert. Today he has brought guitars, because we have always played guitars. It is our one connection besides literature. We sit in one of the parlors with the overstuffed sofas and we jot down lyrics. He teaches me his songs, and I teach him a few of mine. We play; we sing.

"How is your brother?" he asks at last, between numbers.

"He's dying, Keith."

He nods, tunes a guitar string. He has surmised as much, by what I've told him so far. "You wrote that last song for him."

"No, I didn't."

"Certainly, you did. Read that verse."

> *There you are again*
> *Like the first spring*
> *As though we both had grown no older*
> *But time is a thief,*

153

He brings no relief
The look back is much colder,
So much colder

I explain that I wrote the song before I had found out about my brother's condition.

"It doesn't matter *when* you found out," he says. "You knew. At some level, you already knew."

I don't know what I knew. I recall that for a year or so in the early morning hours when I count the ones I love silently to myself and wish good things for them, I included Lee, always wondering what had become of him, and where he was, what his life was like. And while there is a poetically satisfying resonance to Keith's appraisal of the situation, it might more aptly be chalked up to his aesthetic approach to life in general rather than to any facts concerning musical authorship, or spiritual awareness.

•

Martha had noticed he had grown thin, she said, and he had begun to come out of his room less often, sometimes not even to eat. Either she or her daughter would call him up or else rap on his door to see if he needed anything. They would sometimes bring him food when he was too ill to get up to get any for himself, and he always asked for something bland, like rice or applesauce. She'd see him out walking his dog, smoking, always with a quick smile and a kind word. "If he saw that someone was down, he'd try to pick them up somehow," is the way she put it. This is Martha, a down-to-earth woman of rural background. She manages the motel where Mark lives; she knows him as *Mark*. He has been there about six months, and on that last day there she convinced him to let her call an ambulance for him. It had got to the point where he had to struggle to get a breath.

She told me some of this over the phone before I left for Florida, and she recounts some of it now, in a hospital waiting room, filling in details along the way if I happen to ask a question. She is very kind, instinctively compassionate, and her daughter, about twenty years old, has come to the hospital with her, and adds her own observations about my brother. He never missed work. Never. Always was with that dog.

"But his car is still in the drive, and we don't have a key. We've been all through his room, but we can't find it." They are concerned that the battery will die.

I say that most likely he brought the car key to the hospital with him, and now it is probably locked away with the rest of his personal belongings, his watch, his clothes, his wallet.

"Could you ask them for us?"

Sure, sure I can. Then the daughter says, "Did you see him squeeze my finger when I touched his hand tonight? He's so much stronger than he was a few days ago. He's gonna come through. I know he's gonna come through."

Her mother nods in agreement. Oh, yes. He's going to be fine.

There must be red Kryptonite in the room. They don't know? Can't they see it with their own eyes? Being positive, that's very nice, constructive. But it's not helpful at all to deny what is real, what is plain for all to see. I want to tell them, "*No, he's not going to come through. He's not going to make it. He's going to die, and he's going to do it very, very soon, possibly before you leave tonight.*"

My wife can read my thoughts. She touches my hand with hers. I telescope back to a night so clear in my memory it might have been yesterday. After the divorce, we had grown accustomed to seeing our father only on Saturdays when he'd pick us up and take us to various places that divorced men took their children—bowling alleys, golf driving ranges, movies. Lee always sat in the middle of the car's front seat. He was the smallest. I rode shotgun. Pecking

155

order.

One night after being brought home from one of our dad's visits, Lee woke me up late, beyond midnight. His covers thrown back carelessly, he sat on the edge of his bed. "I had a nightmare," he said.

"Everyone has nightmares," I said.

"No, this one was *real*. It seemed like it really happened." He sounded as though he could barely catch his breath.

We had been out riding in Dad's car, pretty much the way we had spent that Saturday, driving down residential streets, laughing, the radio on in the background. All at once Dad and I had vanished, the car had come to an abrupt stop, and both doors were wide open. Everything was still and the sky grew dark. Lee, still sitting on the car seat alone, looked for us, but we were nowhere to be found. Suddenly a deep, horrific voice bellowed from the sky, informing him of what exactly had happened: "*Gagger violence silence*!" it resonated, rolling across the countryside like thunder.

"That doesn't make any sense," I told him. "Go back to sleep."

But he couldn't. He just sat on the edge of his bed trembling. Even then, at that young age, I felt the implications of that vision, of those horrible sounding words. Lee had glimpsed his own isolation, and the frightening, sad truth of it. He'd read the future, had it visited upon him during his sleep, when more fortunate boys dreamed of slamming homeruns or rollicking in imaginary fields.

I think of that night so long ago as I look back at Martha and her young daughter sitting there in the waiting room. I do not shout the truth at them. I swallow it away. They mean no harm.

●

My time in Florida has run out. I must return to the college, go back home to my life. My wife and I make one final visit to the hospital before driving to the airport. The ICU rooms have large windows so the nurses can monitor all the patients from their station. I see before we are even halfway down the corridor that my brother is comatose and back on the ventilator. A nurse catches up to us.

"He had a turn for the worse last night."

Respiratory failure again. The machine inflates his lungs metronomically. At the end of every cycle his body shudders. My wife puts her hand on my back and tells me, "Go ahead. Go see him."

This time I am told by the staff to wear a mask, for Mark's sake, they say, not mine. I do not know why I did not have to wear a mask all those other times. I fit the mask in place and open the door. The machine is noisy, rocks him there in the bed. I have been advised by several people about what to say in this eventuality. I'm supposed to tell him it's all right to let go, that he needn't hold on anymore. Tell him to go toward a light, if he sees one. I don't even know if he can hear me. He's unconscious. But they say maybe.

He looks strangely young in his fragile state, as though he's ready to start all over again.

The ventilator whooshes, lifts his head slightly, exhales once more. He is gone from me. I touch his arm and it feels lifeless already, as if death is not so much a single event as a series of stages. He is more dead today than he was yesterday. Julia has been sent for. She has agreed to do what I legally cannot, to sign a DNR order. She is willing to accept the liability, because this is just cruel. This is not right.

Beneath the surgical mask I whisper, "Buddy. Buddy, can you hear me?" Up and down his head rocks, his body shakes. I don't know if I believe in the idea of a spiritual light. I don't know what I believe. I had always worried about leaving him on his own, and here he is, leaving me. "I was the one who left your bike in the driveway, buddy. It was me. I'm sorry. It was a great bike, a beautiful bike."

It was deep burgundy and had black handlebar grips, a three-speed gearshift. The wheels were polished chrome and coruscated as they spun. I felt safer on it, closer to the ground, you see, less likely to get hurt in a spill. I'd had such a successful ride that morning, really the first good bike ride of my life, that I was in too damned much of a hurry to flip the kickstand down and put it away properly as I should have—just let it drop in front of the garage, and then ran in the house without ever coming to a stop, propelled by the kind of momentum and ebullience youth seemed to generate all on its own.

That was back before any of the world's cares had really touched us, and there was excitement and purity in almost every second of every day. The sky was bluer, and the grass greener, the air so sweet. We were kids. We were just kids.

James Campbell
On Life Support

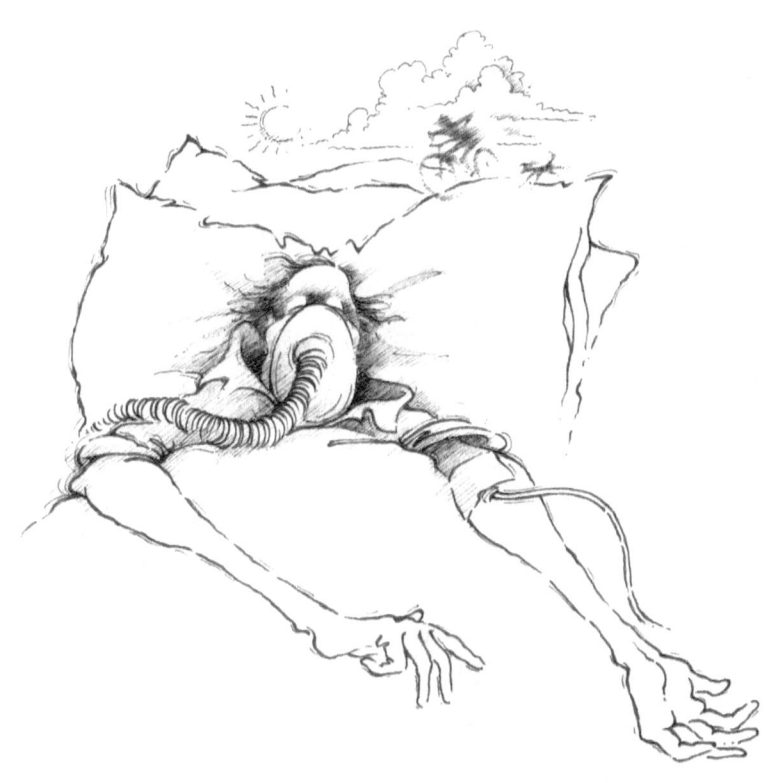

Steve Kowit

Notice

This evening, the sturdy Levis
I wore every day for over a year
& which seemed to the end in perfect condition,
suddenly tore.
How or why I don't know,
but there it was — a big rip at the crotch.
A month ago my friend Nick
walked off a racquetball court,
showered,
changed out of his shorts,
& halfway home collapsed & died.
Take heed you who read this
& drop to your knees now & again
like the poet Christopher Smart
& kiss the earth & be joyful
& make much of your time
& be kindly to everyone,
even to those who do not deserve it.
For although you may not believe it will happen,
you too will one day be gone.
I, whose Levis ripped at the crotch
for no reason,
assure you that such is the case.
Pass it on.

David R. Poe

How It Works

Going to check for mail on a bright October morning, I pause a moment outside our house in Normandy. Across the road, down behind a thatch-roofed house belonging to our dear friend Jacques, flows the Seine, right to left, toward the English Channel. The Seine is an estuary here, and at this moment the tide is rushing in, making the river run backward. Riding the tide inland toward Rouen is a container ship, stacked with metal boxes full of who knows what commitments. It's so massive I can see its top layer glide over Jacques' rooftop. A typical Norman thatch, his roof is capped with a row of plants, mostly irises, rooted in tightly packed clay that seems never to erode. Though we didn't think to imagine it when my wife and I bought this place, also in October years ago, we watched next spring as the irises blazed purple, making the passing of a container ship seem all the more surreal.

From the mailbox near the side of the road, I retrieve a letter I've been expecting and go seat myself in a chair on our front terrace. I open the envelope and remove the results of a blood test I recently had in Paris. My eyes flit quickly down a column listing a small sample of my blood's make up.

Bingo. Amylase. 329. I'm not alarmed, but disappointed. Next to my 329 are numbers indicating healthy levels of amylase. 30-110. At very best, I'm still three times over that.

On a Thursday six weeks ago in Paris, the pain began. Abdominal at first, it spread after two days to my back and chest. My nights were feverish and sweaty, and I vomited anything I ate or drank. My wife was on a work trip in Stockholm and our fourteen-year-old son told me I didn't look well. Sunday morning I arranged for him to stay with friends, left a note for my wife due home that evening, and checked into the American Hospital of Paris. I knew what the pain meant, for I had suffered two bouts of acute pancreatitis before, both times admitting myself to a hospital in Normandy.

By comparison, the American Hospital was a luxury hotel. Single room (I don't think they have doubles), tasteful décor, and doctors who understand English. In Normandy, I had found translating my pain and symptoms into French somehow once removed from the truth, but here at the American Hospital I was practically loquacious and cheery. In no time, they had me in a frock, riding on a gurney, an IV inserted, feeding me crystal clear nourishment I couldn't vomit and—more importantly—painkillers. They took X-rays, did a CAT scan, inserting me prone and feet first through a whirring metal donut as a hot, strangely enticing, liquid coursed through my body. Back in my room, I was excited to catch Andre Agassi on TV, playing in the last tennis match he would ever win, since he would lose two days later in his career's finale.

Our good friend Barb stopped by. She's a doctor at the hospital, working the emergency room. Her youngest son is a schoolmate of our son, her husband one of my best buddies. Though she was aware of my pancreatic history, we chatted like two Americans bumping into each other at a Paris café. Before leaving she gave me a handful of pages, instructing more as a doctor than a chum, "Read this carefully."

Indeed I did. An article from MayoClinic.com on pancreatitis. How it works. The pancreas secretes digestive enzymes and also insulin. Pancreatitis occurs when an overabundance of these enzymes—amylase for one—backs up into the organ itself and begins to digest it. Repeated attacks—I was in the throes of my third in four years—can cause irreparable damage. MayoClinic.com speaks of serious, life threatening complications: infection, pseudocysts, abscesses, shock, kidney, lung or heart failure, and—if one survives those—diabetes and pancreatic cancer. The causes of pancreatitis can stem from environment, genes or just plain gluttony, but the cause that leaped out at me was "excessive alcohol intake." Of course I had been warned of this before, from doctors at the hospital in Normandy and from my GP in Paris.

In English from the Mayo Clinic, "pancreatitis" sounded closer to home. Still, two readings of the article had the ring of a news bulletin issued by the likes of Monty Python. Picture a young John Cleese. "In the Pancreatic War today, angered Amylase, driven into battle once too often by their power-intoxicated leader, rebelled and devoured him." Slapstick news right there in my gut.

Now, sitting on our front terrace with blood results in hand, I am faced with the prospect of a battle longer than I want to admit. I've not sipped a drink in six weeks, but the amylase still rebels. In the hospital my enzyme level had registered over 900. If 100 is normal, 329 has to seem encouraging, and patience a virtue. An English friend up the road who has great tufts of gray hair sprouting from his nostrils is a doctor specializing in acupuncture. He told me I should quit drinking for a year and let my pancreas heal. "If the inflammation scars the pancreas, it'll no longer produce digestive enzymes. You'll have to take about eight enzyme tablets with every meal. And the pain--you ain't felt nothing yet. Probably get hooked on high-octane pain pills. Any alcohol whatsoever will be out of the question." We two have knocked down plenty of wine together, so his advice was tough, he knew. A few years back, he had easily cured my stubborn sciatica with one serving of his magic needles. The jury, he said, was still out on treating pancreatitis with acupuncture and he couldn't recommend it.

I rise and face our house.

It is 225 years old. My wife and I bought it in 1990. Having lived five years in a Paris apartment, we sought a weekend refuge, a *residence secondaire*. More the size and feel of a large cottage, the house is typically mid-to-lower class Norman, one story plus attic—*grenier*, half-timbered. In between the columns a mesh of branches pried into place holds a blend of mud and straw, finished off by a smooth mortar-like mix. The roof is slate, though originally it would have been thatch. There is a foundation of limestone and flint stone, two feet high. The house is narrow and long, probably the lasting influence of early Viking—Norsemen—settlers, who were also boat builders.

Our house. This boat. This vessel. I have poured my soul into it. I was born in Buffalo, NY, and my upbringing had informed me early of do-it-yourself necessity. For various reasons I had always worked on various houses, though never one of my own, and everything I'd ever learned about how an abode worked seemed prelude to a passion I instantly felt when I first saw this Norman fixer-upper. I am now 55 years old, and the notion of having a vessel that contains my soul is intriguing. For fifteen years I have sawed, sanded, drilled, plumbed, wired, tiled, roofed, floored, cemented, mortared, spackled, painted and varnished. Our house is built into a gradual slope that pays homage to the Seine. I have pushed the earth behind us back. One weekend two buddies—an Austrian and an Australian my wife worked with—and I shoveled out a ton of dirt. I have spent hours and hours rummaging through used-lumber yards, measuring tape in hand, seeking just the right oak beam. My two favorite beams, running five meters lengthwise in the dining room I've added, originate from an old hospital in Rouen. It took me three days to strip them of a dozen coats of oil paint. It is surprising that deposits of leaden dust never showed up in my CAT scan.

My work at first was eyed suspiciously by the neighbors, who probably feared I'd slap on aluminum siding. "These Americans, they think they can go anywhere and do anything." But I have stayed true to the Norman half-timbered style, for it was love at first sight. I hanker for the sight, smell and feel of wood. Ironically, there was very little visible wood when we bought the house. Everything inside had been plastered over during a strange trend in the 20's and 30's that valued concealing a Norman house's skeletal wood. Probing with a mere pen knife, I discovered that a good deal of the lower beams along the front of the house, the north side that gets sun only in summer, had succumbed to rising damp, and rotted away. As needed, someone had gouged out the rot and whacked in cement, then plastered over everything and painted on chocolate stripes where the beams would be. I stripped it all back, my nostrils full of the odor of damp and rot. I found cozy dens full of sleepy woodlice. I spliced in necessary sections of oak and replaced a foundation of rubble and clay with waterproofing, clean-cut stone and mortar.

When I wasn't in Paris—teaching or editing or raising our son—I was in Normandy. Sometimes, when I couldn't write in Paris, I comforted myself at home, where it was easier to knock out a wall than a short story.

While knocking out much of the wall space on the house's south side, I always cleaned up and left intact any original beams that didn't absolutely need replacing. I have added a dining room and, carving into the slope, a two-story addition with a recreation room and bathroom downstairs, and an office and full bath upstairs. Between the dining room and the rec room is a small bar—a slab of recycled oak and barstools from IKEA. Since these additions face south, I have installed as much glass as possible to let in the sunlight that rolls down our slope. It took eight of us (mostly locals who by then had learned to trust me) one sunny Saturday to raise the beams for the two-story bit. Sometimes, when I gaze on, even run my fingers over, our house's original beams and joint work, I can imagine a group of Normans years ago raising beams.

My village friends and I had done a modern impression, using Skil, Bosch, and Black-and-Decker power tools. *Sans électricité*, our predecessors, Amish-like, had sawed and drilled by hand, pegging together tenon-and-mortise joints. We had used steel angles and bolts, later made invisible once I had filled in the walls. I sometimes think the long-deceased Normans watch me the way I have watched them. "Hey, Pierre," one shouts. "Come look what the American is concocting now!"

My wife and I have convinced our son never to sell the house. He promises he won't, whatever a fourteen-year-old's promise is worth. (I promise more homework, less computer, a clean room, shampooed hair). In any case, I can say this: our son has an aptitude for this house. His understanding of how it works is turning into affection. We save money for his college education, but if he becomes a plumber, mason, carpenter, we will be proud. His attentive eye and do-it-yourself dexterity reassure me. Maybe he senses, when I explain electricity or plumbing to him, I am purposely imparting the know-how he'll need to maintain this place when I am no longer around.

When I am no longer around. How my soul used to rage against the thought. Rage against the dying of the light—though I was only twenty. In those days of "Nietzsche is peachy," I was the existential hippie, full of Sartre's *Nausée* and Kierkegaard's *Fear and Trembling.* As much as the angst hurt, it was cool. Many years later, the novelist Jane Smiley would put a new name to it, "The Age of Grief," though her version of it attacks people in their 30s. She wonderfully evokes the image of Christ in Gethsemane, sweating blood and begging heaven, "Lord, if it by thy will let this cup be lifted." But it cannot be lifted, and the cup comes round for each of us to drink from. My own age of grief smoldered a long time, but in the last few years it has subsided. My only nausée these days comes from pancreatitis. Maybe I simply seek a resignation with dignity. Maybe I am consoled by this house, my soul's vessel, which will be tended to by our son.

Fifty-five years old, I can still throw a football that many yards, though I can't imagine that clean age-to-distance ratio holding up even another year. When not threatened by rebellious amylase, I feel I could really enjoy another twenty-year stretch of highway. But I know how it works at this age. My wife and I have watched close friends, more or less our age, die, four to cancer (two other friends have beaten it), and one to heart attack. The last was overweight and diabetic, and in that strange, I dare say, smug way people can have even toward dear friends, we saw it coming. Also, about the time I was fretting turning fifty, I received word that a woman I had lived with after we'd graduated college and traveled cross country in an old Dodge van, had died of a heart attack, leaving behind a husband and two children. I hadn't seen her in twenty-five years, and quite frankly our own relationship had been a mismatch, but remembering her washing dishes in a Wyoming stream, I felt the clear jolt of the unexpected. So, as long and pleasant as that last stretch of highway might look, there is occasionally a sudden great patch of black ice. Trouble is, there's no road under the ice.

I guess I was attracted to women who love to travel.

My wife and I have traveled the world for twenty-three years, beginning with Greece soon after we met. We have made love on every continent but Antarctica. Back then, while I lusted after literature, she was becoming a PhD economist. These past two decades her work for an organization in Paris has allowed her wide travel, and much of the time our son and I are with her in the seats we three have in exchange for the business class she gives up. These days we are often stopped at airport security checks, and she once again must produce the doctor's letter explaining the syringe in her purse. For a dozen years she's injected herself twice daily, pricked her finger three or four times daily, and slipped a paper strip into her portable glucose reader. One time we were on a cruise ship, sitting around a dining table with friends, having to wait much too long for food after my wife's injection. She began shaking and sweating, her eyelids fluttering. While I coaxed bread and beer into her mouth, a friend swept our crying son away. That's the only time such a thing has happened. As far as I know. For my wife is not the kind of person to talk about her troubles.

Besides a love of travel, my wife and I share a love of wine. Wine nurtured our love for each other. One of our shared heartbreaks is the theft of wine from our Paris cellar, and we know that makes us fortunate by comparison. We have sat a thousand times on our terrace out front drinking wine, watching the Seine flow, ships pass. In summer, when the garden's in bloom, we look at our roses, toast each other and joke, "To the days of wine and roses." Because of our property's slope, the front terrace actually sits atop a garage at the roadside. On nice days we often call down to passersby--the village is small, about sixty people--to come join us for a glass of wine. We have the only roadside terrace in town and so it has become something of a drinking dais.

Our village is named Vieux Port, so called because the Romans had a port here. Bacchus would have loved this town, where the wine flows as sure as the Seine. Most of the houses now are *secondaire*, whose owners—Parisian, English, Dutch—come to kick back on weekends, during holidays, much as we have done, though we spend the most time here beside the *permanents*, and will soon retire and live full time in Vieux Port. The locals enjoy us *étrangers*, not just because we pump money into the economy, but maybe because we connect them to the eccentric world. A few here have never even seen Paris. In this village everything flows—the talk, laughter, music. In summer barbecues smoke and in winter fireplaces blaze. We never tire of watching the Seine, our river that starts as a trickle in Burgundy. Till recently, everyday at precisely 11:31, the Concorde—on its way to New York, where it would land three hours before it took off—streaked over our heads, several miles up, and by the time you heard it you had to look quickly along its vapor trail to actually see it. Every four years, a majestic armada of tall ships gathers at Rouen. Then, always on a Sunday, they sail one after another down the Seine, bearing flags from around the world, past Vieux Port whose population that day swells to a thousand. Some ten miles upstream, in the town of Villequier, Victor Hugo watched from the shore one day as his daughter, son-in-law and another couple, their boat capsized by a sudden storm, drowned. A statue of the great man stands on the bank, his head downcast, and beneath are written his words, "the grass lives and the children die."

In 1945 the Germans were pinned down in Vieux Port, back in the days when the village had a number of *auberges* serving food and drink, and the Germans, too, used Vieux Port for rest and relaxation. (The auberges, tainted perhaps, disappeared after the war, never to return. I keep meaning to write a story based on the German presence here. The villagers old enough to have lived through it have never brought it up, and I have never inquired. But I do wonder what went on behind doors we so easily pass through these days.) From the flat farmland above the woods, the English fired a few shells, just to remind the Germans the war was nearly over and they really should be on their way. One shell hit the house next to ours, killing the resident, whose name is on a plaque at the church, where a number of us gather on VE day. Next to the cemetery that surrounds the church someone decided to place the green bin where we recycle our bottles, clink-clank, and after some weekends or holidays the bin overflows. My wife and I plan on being buried in Vieux Port, within earshot of the bottle bin.

Up behind our property, behind a field—which some absentee landlord lets to grazing horses who get occasional carrots or apples from our son and his friends at our split-rail fence—is forest, mostly beech trees. Hidden there you find the ruins of the 12th century *Chapelle de Saint Thomas*, where lepers would pray. It is built on the site of a Roman temple, though no one knows to whom it was dedicated. I vote for Bacchus. It is a charmed life we lead in charming Normandy. Ah, Vieux Port! Ah, Veritas Partytown!

I am sitting at our dining room table, drinking tea, *orange canelle* with the slightest suggestion of spice, indeed a superior vintage. In the past six weeks I have found different flavors of tea and infusions interesting. Alas, the tastes of currants or vanilla gotten from a brewed bag will never replace those of fine wines. I sip, read from one of the many articles on pancreatitis I've downloaded since first discovering MayoClinic.com. I've come to think the alcohol aspect a bit overplayed, at times preachy. While my own choices are beer or wine, some people around here knock down vodka, whiskey, gin, and have no apparent problems, though some pancreases evidently are more delicate than others. Now I'm reading the news I somehow have been waiting for. The University of Maryland Medical Center gives the usual spiel how alcohol not only hastens enzyme output, but then, with a follow-up punch, allows those juices to pass more easily through duct walls and damage the pancreas. But umm.com turns upbeat, speaking of things that are actually good for your pancreas. Anti-oxidants, like soybean extracts, may be beneficial, and certain traditional Chinese medicines "are effective for the prevention and treatment of pancreatitis": licorice root, ginger root, Asian ginseng, peony root, cinnamon Chinese bark. I knew it! Ah, pancreas, heal thyself that I may drink my wines again!

Just because I can repair sinks and toilets, am I daft enough to think I can repair a leaky pancreas? ("Pass the duct tape, son.") The last doctor who treated me at the American Hospital, a Frenchman who amazingly had done his residency in Cleveland, Ohio—and so could relate to Buffalo winters—told me my pancreas was a keg of dynamite ready to go off. I didn't admonish him for clichés. My French GP in Paris, perhaps whose *joie de vivre* hasn't been chilled by a stay in Cleveland, says, sure, once the enzyme level returns to normal, I can have a few glasses of wine now and then. That's not bottles per day, as so easily happens around here. Control, moderate your intake. Drink only nice wines, not the stuff on sale we all buy just because it's cheap fuel for conversation and laughter.

Still, there is that other voice of late. Quit. Just give it up.

You know and admire a number of ex-alcoholics—no one from this town, of course—and they converse and laugh with gusto and wit.

This table came with the house. It's made of simple planks, I think beech, and seats six easily, more with some squeezing. Hundreds of meals we've eaten here, with so many guests and friends, as the wine and chatter flowed. What's most interesting about this table are the small markings in it, as though someone spilled a box full of apostrophes across it. According to the previous owner, the table came from a WWII German mess tent, and the markings were made by knife tips. The owner said he and his wife bought the table in Germany and transported it here. I've always found that odd, and I wonder if that's because the owner found it less—what? Scary? Discomforting?—than telling us new homeowners the table was here all along, that Nazi soldiers sat in our house, at this table, stabbing at their food.

Tonight we have Françoise and Renald coming for dinner. My wife is making duck breasts. She is easily the best cook in town, and I'll bet one of the best in Normandy. We will break out bottles of older *Châteauneuf du Pape*, instead of the average stuff, for this particular couple appreciates good wine. I will make my little joke of late. "None for me. Why, I'm so far ahead of you all, I gotta give you a chance to catch up."

I hear my wife and son returning from Pont Audemer, the nearest town with a supermarket, and must help unload the car.

My wife and I don't talk to each other as much as we used to, and it would be easy lately to blame my lack of drink, but it is bigger, something that has been happening for I'm not really sure how long. I must remember to explain to our son how love works. You fall into it full of passion, my boy, discovering so much to share. You get married, have a kid or two, hopefully as fine as you. Then twenty-three years down the road you find yourselves tiptoeing around each other some days, sharing only the most necessary information: what goes on the shopping list, the fact the vacuum bag needs changing, and the guests arrive at seven. By day, you accuse each other of snoring the night before. Sometimes you think her stoicism expresses itself as impatience with other people's problems. She goes around turning lights on, you turning them off. She thinks you enjoy agonizing over choices rather than simply making decisions (maybe an old existential hippie does). You think she buys distractions too readily for your son. She thinks you have a pretentious chip on your shoulder. You think maybe you do, a great big Buffalo chip. Your master bedroom, in the only house the two of you will ever own, feels more and more like Antarctica. Still, you know you are lucky because in the guest bedroom, on the top shelf of the armoire, there are seventeen albums of photos, most of which you have shot but your wife has put in order and labeled.

The groceries are stowed away, sunlight fills the kitchen, and my wife begins snipping the ends off green beans. It's a beautiful kitchen I've built for her. Oak cabinets, black granite countertops with small gold speckles, a range, two big ovens, and a microwave. A spotlighted island chopping table in the middle and lights in the ceiling made from some leaded windows with touches of red and gold I found cheap in an Amsterdam flea market.

There is a sudden *crack!* and I know instantly what it is. Once in awhile a bird, its eye unable to distinguish between reality and reflection, slams into one of the many windows I've installed and breaks its neck. "We need to stick on some do-not-enter decals," my wife says and I enjoy her words. This time it's a blackbird, its body warm through the paper towel as I carry it up to a barrel we keep for the likes of pulled weeds and deadheaded roses. When the barrel's full I drive it up to a big recycling yard where there's a giant bin for *déchets verts*. They turn it all into mulch, and in the spring I can get a few free barrels to sprinkle around the rosebushes. I look at our house.

One hundred years from now, perhaps a great-grandchild, curious to know what life was like back then, will read my stories searching for clues. Two hundred years from now I don't know that my words will be read. But I do know this. Someone will walk around this house and wonder how these beams have stood so long. Even during the shortest days of the year, the sun will roll its light down the slope, across the field, through a few bare apple trees, in through the glass wall, across a bar and into the kitchen, where it finds a woman happily preparing food, though in the back of her mind is the slight worry that her husband really needs to change the bag before he starts vacuuming.

James Campbell

Alleluia

Jack Marshall

Sunny Days

Midday as in late summer, though it's barely
Early March, and with the velvety rustle of little
More than skin-and-bone-wings, a warbler
Wolf-whistles the blue loveliness above.

In Berkeley, the sidewalk outside the cafe is the color
Of the sky. I'm soaking up the sunshine, lapping
A latte, tasting the flakiest croissant au chocolat
In what may be my last meal toward the end

Of the era of unchecked power of the Western World,
While a cherry-sweet chirping in the trees is clearing
Throats of winter. Today, throats are better off
In Berkeley than in Baghdad,

Where in one form or another heat hits
Like a stroke, even where a car-roadside-or-human
Bomb has not. There are so many
Sunny days for Death in Baghdad.

The sky above here, as there, though limitless
Beneath which we pray not to suffer
What is made with so much space
To suffer in, is not big enough for me

To feel what a mother must feel
On the street as she turns on her heel
At the sound of danger to her children;
Or before sending one out

For the day's bread, knowing it could cost
The life of one who breathed

In, through, out of you.

Just this morning, taking a hot shower, I heard,
"This is as close as you will get to being with
Your mother again," and for a second forgot
What dimension I would step out into.

Fast fatiguing, fitful sleeping,
Urgent peeing, eyesight dimming,
Are not good omens for hope,
Since all our hopes suppose

We'll live them healthy.

Instead, a person across the sea
Nightly crumbles before our eyes,
Laying his head like a heart in a vise
For the handler's pleasure.

The weight of multitudes and their gods:
I hate the weight of the gods
Of multitudes, but love heaven's
Silken silence leaving no trail

But sunset's crimsoning sail.

Light dims; cats doze; birds start up their din.
This is the hour I like best, which slides
Slow as a veil over a ravishing creature's thigh,

Who will ravish again tomorrow.

Family and self-preservation aside, my worst fear
In the doomsday scenarios I'm given to lately
Is a quake, nuclear, or terrorist attack,
In which my seven cats scatter

To the four winds; creatures so high-strung,
And still, they're lordly and lethal at once,
Yet whose squinting eyes pain makes
Even the kitten's frightened face shrunken, old.

Where to, then, who have never known anywhere
But home? First, let me sweep the stones
From their path, and pray their killing
Skills thrive on living smells in the grass.

For us, there's the astronomical
Luck in the starlight not stopping.

Jack Marshall

Dimming

There is a glacier, grown slowly as hair,
dissolving faster than our thoughts
run past. There is one's self, close

to being absent at any moment, and all
of us under a sign in an unknown season
we know for certain we'll be dying,

when loved ones will vanish, and we
unable to hold or kiss or ever miss them again.

Besides warming, there's the double whammy
of global dimming: obstructed solar rays
the red rim on the blackening tin twilight is riding,

like the slowed down sweeping of a grain
of glucose firing through the brain, the way
memory comes from, goes into, and through

what we feel, and becomes the real;
like the past, inventing itself in the last second
I keep coming back to the places that keep

coming from the sunset I am a student of
at my desk, where every seat is a front-row seat;
the vast red vapor trail erasing the horizon

against which time narrows and place deepens
in the clarity of outline, in the last light.

I am a student of sinking that lasts
seconds, and of which I am a part, and
do not follow. The longer I fail, the longer

I live. To live, I fail; I fail, and live
in the furrows of feelings that live
in the places we lived in, empty now

of us and what we did there,
with failing faith, failed friends, in moments
that were loved, in hours that weren't.

Lennox Raphael

Joy 0f Age

"If I had known I was going to live this long,
I would have taken better care of myself."
—Eubie Blake, who lived to 100

What therefore is age, or aging; knowing it happens every day, each moment, is happening now, we know, and, yet, we seldom take notice until (sometimes) too late; and, alas, we become question marks; and, in this sense, while age, a pop commercial construct sold in malls and pharmacies, remains companionable, as fear and blessing, blushing as middle-aged rainbows, one is never ever different from any other person, and, although we may not think of death, or even slowly dying of the hobble gobble hobble of being destined to be babies again, and have probably fooled ourselves into seeing immortality as a process of language and art, it is revenge that keeps one going, revenge against time, a rebirth of the spirit in dying alive between the lines of no return; and, yet, of course, one may be too old to be trusted; or, perhaps, old enough to be ignored; yet never believed; but by whom, certainly not by the messenger who insists no photograph fades, particularly the photographs of ourselves as, fleeing the horrors of life, its pleasures, and the promise of passage into butterfly wings, we disappear into the essence of our being; but, never despair; wonder is too precious a thing to be lost on regret: you are you, and no other: not the pre-ghost, or prosthetic deceit: and I am me, too; and the 'no other' is the mirror image of youth, our youthfulness as age-thinking, and those memories of aging & growing old, and older still, and the effort to restructure our focus and escape comfortable traps of body regret while, as willing participants in the joy of age, enjoying life and resisting being victims of the history of the body: or even the mind; especially our minds; remembering today is also yesterday's future of speculative becoming: the same for everyone, man/woman; so, it's true, perhaps even as a warning, when memories weep we do have to wet our dreams; we have to free ourselves from the ice of those memories: and move on, acknowledging we have lived for writing, and are glad to be old as we are, as I am now, old as we have always been; glad that age, for me, as for you, is a dream come true; although I never guessed it would be this difficult, these pages about age, as supposed to be, the appreciation of age, the age of wine, age of our dreams, old age: we never speak of young age: and I am so disappointed, in myself, that it has taken me so long to describe my intentions when I started writing JOY OF AGE, really not knowing what it meant, or even the feeling of it, having no answers, but starting out from the premise (and conviction) that age is personal, with all the meanings of this lone word, a journey that only one person (the you in me and we) experiences in the self, internally, dismissing the look, the outerness of age, how one looks, in the transformation/deconstruction of appearances, to oneself, and to others, in (these) times beyond the wrinkle-proof reflections of our lives; so, Age, I am discovering, is a process of memory rather than actuality, and it is memory that sustains the image of the self and props up our bones and their cultural positioning, and also takes us thru squalor & innocence down the road of reincarnative fantasies; of course, this is an unfinished piece, exploring the Augean stable of Age as myth, endless, incurable, always under construction, our lives; my life; yours; we think centuries: before & after; which keeps us going: not how we look/feel, or the fact one set out to alphabetize the joys of age: from A to Z, from ending to beginning: how, to begin with, age, for me, as is everything else in this piece, has always been a simple

181

thing, a careless curiosity; and, in many ways, as I approach the golden paradise of 70, awesomely beautiful, the emotional excavation continues, as does the inherited memory of being a wartime child from September ⊠39, yet, in myself, feeling healingly peaceful; which has always been my meditation: that the joy of age for me be the way I feel right now, this spring of 2007, living in Copenhagen, born in Trinidad (Tobago), having lived in countries, such as Brazil, Morocco, Puerto Rico, the United States, now almost 15 years in Scandinavia, and almost the same time in Manhattan, during the sixties & seventies; and this living , and being, and influenced always by friends older than myself; and by some much younger, taking my cue of life always from memories of the conviction of belonging to a world family—however invisible at times; and have dated myself according to my writing, as a measurement of achievement, and of longing for bliss, remembering the visions of self, at age 6, deciding I wanted to be a writer; and embarking on a living as one soon after my 18th birthday, and never once stopping; dating myself by my writing, my ambition for the craft, and believing from early on it was holy, that one did better work as one became a better person, a strong belief, which still buoys me, that my understanding of life and its deeper implications will infuse the work with a simplicity and uniqueness beyond the imagination of time taken for granted; and, beginning with an awareness of standards and respect for the tradition, and for the work done by one's peers and others; so my age is really in my writing; and I can tell how old I am, and how old I would have to become, by the progress I detect in my work, which is language and translation of the imagined impossible made simple by a clear observation of the inner environment; yet, again, as man, I am not too sure, because age is more importantly a process of thinking, how we think of ourselves; how we think ourselves thru the rapids of beauty, and I am too respectful of women to believe that they age differently in the elegance of themselves; sure, I know that beauty is popularly more than skin deep &, if we listen to the slogans, and we are supposed to be what we eat, what we drink, how we relate to the world and media-induced stress, and those measurements provided by reflections of our shared institutions and communities, especially when coming from our friends and close relationships; but Age, yes, with a capitalized a, personally speaking, after all these years of leading up to the youthfulness of 80, I still don't know what it is, and, in this respect, consider myself a day-to-day expert; and, then, what is my day like: I write often 50 or so words a day, at whatever time of the day, but mostly late night: today, for example, I went swimming in the sea at 7; something I do every morning, have been doing all my life, except for those more than ten years I lived in Manhattan; with the only difference that here, in Denmark, the water is considered (by others) bitter cold most of the year; yet, for me, well, I don't think about it, and swimming when below zero, or even under the ice, is a fond meditation; so some, who know of this, would say to me, "No wonder you look so fresh!" :but it is more than this, more than the freshness of a breeze in the soul, more than the fact I eat neither fish, meat nor eggs and drink sparingly and fast often; and love jokes, even a friend exclaiming at the birth of my daughter, Papaya, now 10, *"O, my God, Lennox, you're making your grandchildren."* : yes, I can enjoy the joke: *"What do you do?"* asked another, *"have you made a pact with the devil?"*: no, no, no, I haven't; not yet, at least; I am just too busy catering to the positive in the unknown; and, besides, there is only one Dorian Gray; anyhow, what matters is that, suddenly, I am writing this after many jottings and putting off the actual crafting for the longest time, telling myself I would do it next week, then, forgetting, time passes as a ghost, and the very thought of betraying the deadlines ages me considerably in ways that are apparent only from the inside; and even now, out of desperation really, I struggle to illustrate the age journey/adventure, knowing I feel joyful, that I live spiritually, and my genes are constructed of language and have little to do with history/actuality: that, if anything, I inhabit a curious soul and have no fear of life or of the constant reincarnations/inventions within; so where are we now? and should I tell you how, at 40, measuring myself by the age in which my father sat down in the bathroom & never got up, I was deathly afraid I would not live past his 56; and, as tho trapped in an existential duel with time, I began to misdirect my energies and neglect the visionary possibilities of suffering as an art form; but my writing would soon take care of that; so, again, I wonder whether I should write too of the cycling I do, or the regular fasting, or that, after years of having it be my wings, I have fallen out of love of driving a car; or that I've done zazen meditation, since 1967, and yoga, particularly sun salutation, and do lots of walking in the forest every week, even in the snow, and spend two weeks skiing in Norway with my daughter & her mom every year; that I paint a lot and write a lot and read indiscriminatingly and believe in God and family life and community and get by on four to five hours sleep every day, that I have been married four times and have four adult sons, three with kids of their own; boys in Oregon, Miami, LA, Texas; but, still, who am I? am I man, spirit, person, or woman: or all these things including a part of you as I write between the lines? well, should I write then of the lies I told in my youth when I worked on newspapers in various countries and would inflate my age in order to receive larger salaries? should I write of the epic pain two years ago which led eventually to having my gall bladder removed? should I write of the time, years ago, on the break-up of a marriage, with kids involved, when I felt a pain even greater than the gall bladder experience, those early months of the separation when I aged a million years and died a thousand times and was kept alive only by the companionship of writing and the awareness I was yet to fulfill my debt to it? so, age, then: what is it all about? is it just geography of the body or people, when they become aware of the range of things I have done, always asking me—*how old are you?*— *you don't look your age—look at you, you still have mother's milk on your face!—you always look so young—tell me your secret*: and when I tell them my age they think I am putting them on; sometimes therefore, to end the conversation, I say what they want to hear, that I am two score, or less: neglecting to share that I feel myself an ageless spirit that outranks maleness, a patient of Dr. Groucho Marx who prescribes "a man is as old as the woman he feels"; grief relief; however, to get back to the struggle to write about age, one's aging, male-aging, the device of alphabetizing my feelings just did not seem to work; and, now, it is left for you to judge; and, luckily, we know already that, for one thing, practice makes perfect; and the longer you live the longer you see; but all this thinking didn't help with the writing when, finally, I began looking at the alphabet structure I had employed as an escape from spontaneity, starting out, for example, with A: that Age is a number; you are as old as you feel; old as you look; or believe; old as you think; as we refuse to be who you are: Age philosophy: Age as a weapon against time; Age is only a manner of speaking; and, as one grows older, one stops being oneself; we speak of growing old in the Age of Paranoia; Age as the next monster we face around the corner; Age, like color, and gender, becoming a profession if one chooses to pursue it to the detriment of life as wholeness; Age as acceptance: acceptance of the mythology of time, the many levels of its playfulness and counter-reality; well, I've been a number from the get go, my mother saying the first time she laid eyes on me I was lying between two (2) angels; (*"I was talking to your mom today and she said the first time she laid eyes on you you were lying between two angels with wings"*) well, I was hearing this for the first time, and wasn't too surprised because I have always felt protected, and had known all along, even before I could think mythologically, I would have to stop being a thought & accept my destiny of being a myth of Age as style & elegance and how, as men, we perceive ourselves, our destiny, the mythology of our lives; the being of seeing & believing that age is coming to terms with one's responsibility to one's time, and to the hereafter, even while never taking any of these things too seriously, and, yet, canonizing them as being funny at times; and, as one grows older, which is happening, slowly, inordinately, for quite some time now, even before we were able to account fully for ourselves; convinced always Age is personal and, like youth a habit; one man's joy being another's poison; and age, too, being how you feel; and both a question of numbers & being numbered among the silence (and noise) of generations, and I sat alone for months; before I knew what was happening, remembering I was old enough suddenly to be my father's brother; and would one day be older than my father ever was, and old enough to be my grandfather; even as one gets mixed up in dreams and nostalgia; since there is always the temptation to look back: I don't: in fact, I wished only to be tempted to look back more often; just as I am thinking now of how C too; and D: the missing letters of my life; + E & F & G & H; but not I, curiously enough: I don't think age; have never felt old; I am not age; not Age/Mileage/Cleavage; not immortality as the inspirational trick we play on ourselves, forgetting/ ignoring Age is the beast without; we know we are not going to live forever; history proves that; and we are not about to be ungrateful: not the we or you or hidden selves: so I have learnt over the years to accept the responsibility of my imagination; and I write a lot: over the years, loads of manuscripts; have lost novels in manuscript; 2; and, then, one day, I started thinking of age, that I wouldn't be here forever, that I owed it to my work to make an intervention in its growing up, as I did at its birth, that it was time to stop 'hiding' and face—no, no, not face—the time had come to understand how best to misunderstand the things I had written, and then feared, simply because I hadn't the courage to face the fruit and the implications of an imagined wisdom and carelessness: or nonchalance; but we would then discover that age creeps up on you—and one's best response is to creep out of its shadow; that in this business, the grind of close observation and excavating the imagination, and remembering, writing, worrying unnecessarily, cultivating distractions, and being a writer, an artist, dreaming it's the work that lives, that's supposed to be Methuselah; not me, not you; when I am 80 on a sailboat made of green bones: memories: I keep telling myself this; because it is a wish; I have never been a successful sex maniac; that too (and neither you); yet, after 5 kids & 4 marriages, this can easily be disproved; not the fact one is more easily aroused by language & etiquette (good manners): and, in addition to this deflowering of nostalgia, one refuses to believe age is a number, or that one could ever be too old to be trusted; and I wonder sometimes: where would we be without our contradictions; not me; there was a time when I always wanted to be older; that's how I started out, how, from around 10, when I began realizing that older people had something I coveted: a certain *glance* (so no wonder I would love the company of older people) like Kafka's shadow; but where was I all this time? and couldn't I have written *KEEPING THE FAITH IS THE SUREST BAIT?* yes, of course, L would always be easy: Love goes hand in hand with loneliness, and age holds the tail of the pig and allows itself to be dragged across the quicksand; *I am amazed*; yet M, like mother, would always be there: reminding us, metaphorically, age is just a metaphor, and writing, too; and also a life; something I worked out at six when I wanted to be a writer for the rest of my life: and, in later teenaged years, to get through the time peacefully, I would fool my father into believing I could be the lawyer he always wanted me to be, and, when 10 years later, awakening with a start from a dream where I had been wrapped like a mummy in words painted silver and gold, I knew I would, from there on, be too busy writing (as living) to get lost in being the age that others might have been seeking as a Mask; so M had ended with *Mask*; and what was the meaning of this? was age a mask, and life a masquerade?: let's see!; or no man an island, no matter how old, or young.; but, like I've said, I don't think age; not since that wonderful start from the time of my birth on my parents' cocoa estate, and I, knowing Only memories have the power (and insouciance) to age us, don't wish to start all over again; I meet Thomas Kennedy, the writer, here in Copenhagen, and the first thing he says to me is, *"I was expecting to meet a much older person"* or, perhaps, *"I was expecting a much older-looking person."*: nothing strange!; he had been hearing so much of *CHE!*, and *CHE!* had been staged 69-70, in Manhattan, … and here I was, walking thru his front door … and I didn't know what to say; but what went thru my mind as I sat in his living room was the night during *BLUE SOAP*, a musical vaudeville, the second theatre production of my life, which ran for three months in Manhattan, right after *CHE!*, when a celebrated Italian cinematographer stayed behind, after the show, and the first thing he said was, *"O, I'm so surprised. I was expecting to meet a much older person. Your work is so old, and classic!"*: and, again, I didn't know what to say; but that was 1970; and altho many words & images have flowed under the bridge since then, I am still eager to see what Q brought; but a p had somehow strayed out of line: and the word was Pleasure: the pleasure that life, in spite of the pain & joy & surprises, is the one thing worth its weight in dreams: so what then for Q?: just: Quest/Question: and it's too late to add anything to this; and R was Roar like a lion, run like the hare, while S was Sex so what about sex?; and sexy?; even as one continues to thank God for large mercies; and for the help in saying (to age) until death do us part; not knowing, and perhaps not even caring, what age thinks of this, and of course, in no hurry for a reply, and who is? certainly not T standing alone like a grand oak tree; U too; and V was Vanity as a wonderful companion, with nothing about the victory of survival in these times, or W being Writing is my age; and I have always measured this age by the progress of my writing; and have always wanted to be 80; yeah!; not because I'm greedy, not because I want to live to be a hundred; just because I've always known that at 80 I'd be doing my best work; yes, wishes; old wine; and X was simply Xcept: which made me curious to know Y; and Y was you are as young as your imagination; with Z being Zest apart, to a point, we have always wanted to be: older/elder: to have dreams; and that boast about 80 is not me, it's the being inside of us dreaming of the Beginning; the forever now as wish and punishment; that's *that*: the important thing is to have a growing sense of ourselves, and to avoid becoming victims of expectations; for, as we grow older, even while growing younger, time becomes more circular, and things are not simply up and down, or mirrored in absences, or going to bed at 10, up at 2, without the help of an alarm, writing until 5, and, 30 minutes later, after yoga on the beach & fire meditation, having a lovely swim where, turning from opaque grey to purple, to splashes of yellowing red on the surface, the sea makes no effort to resist its gifts—or gloat; and all was quiet & restful and, deservingly, a private timelessness: and the only thought was to the beginning of the morning, and a swan looking back at me as I felt like a baby one more time in your arms; so, there, you have it, a piece as confused, and confusing, as age is at times, but rich, and overflowing with curiosity and vulnerability; reminding me of a very wealthy man, a relative, who, dressed to the hilt, in tails, spends hours each day in his chicken coop, chatting with his chickens; his only complaint being they do not understand him: which I do understand: and my one hope is this not be my fate ... to be misunderstood by my imagination, and to have to rely on growing younger each day in the Age of Paranoia; and I hope you like this too: that the Joy of Age is within reach; and so are we.

George Dickerson

El Gallo's Last Faena

I know this bull;
He is an impudent bull;
I have fought this bull before.

I have seen his dark shoulders
Shadow the eyes of Gypsy girls
Whose lovers caroused to war.

I know this bull;
He is a crazed and careless bull:
He hungered for the soul of Garcia Lorca.

The furnace of this bull's breath
Snorts out ashes; his tongue
Is long as the Guadalquivir.

His great hooves trowel the earth
Until a matador's blood
Flowers the sand.

I know this bull;
This Miura's horns will hook and
Splinter into the satin groin of night.

Not Belmonte or great Joselito,
With their brave veronicas,
Could confuse this bull.

His glare is a surgeon's scalpel
In the harsh hot bullring
Of a reflector's light.

At Granada, at Madrid,
The corrida's tiers are empty;
In *sol y sombra,* no olés resound.

Even my picador has gone.
At exactly five in the afternoon,
I have thrown my banderillas down.

El Gallo knows you, Toro;
My faena is nearly done.
I'm ready, Toro. Hey! Toro! Come!

Nicholas Birns

People Become Parts of This World

It had been a good Thanksgiving. I had spent the day with friends and family and then seen my cousin Steve, a jazz musician, play that night at the Village Vanguard. I came home, logged on to the Internet, and read the *New York Times* web page to check the news. In the lower right corner of the computer screen, I saw the heading, "Dobson, former pitcher, dies at 64." Never as an adult male have I felt the intimations of mortality than I did at that moment. Many athletes I followed when I was a boy have died, but never one with the sort of integral intimacy I felt with Pat Dobson. Dobson was a man I never met in person, but with whom I had as prized a relationship in a psychological sense as any male relative. That this connection, though deep, was not extensive, that it was centered in a few months over thirty years back, in a way sharpened the sting.

I had not really followed what he had been doing recently. But Pat Dobson dying was something else. Was it some sort of anomalous tragedy, or an indication of a whole generation passing? Dobson's onetime manager, Earl Weaver, was still alive at an even older age. But the mourning was mainly performed by men younger than Dobson, who had employed him as a scout and coach: Mike Flanagan of the Orioles, Brian Sabean of the Giants. The death was a shock, but Dobson was at the age where deaths are shocks, but shocks of the sort that can plausibly happen; it is a shock not of the unbelievable variety, but one which arouses the feeling, "Oh no, I'm so sorry that this happened so soon." Dobson had died suddenly, apparently from leukemia, which had only been diagnosed the day before. The disease came on so swiftly it could not be treated, as was the similar case of my former student and friend Annette. It must be tough for Dobson's family and friends to come to terms with such a sudden absence. It was disconcerting even for me, at a far greater remove.

I checked the various places on the Web where I might look for news. Wikipedia, with its grisly collective efficiency, had reliably noted the death; Baseball reference, a huge, authoritative website that more or less seems run by one person, had not yet caught up. To reassure myself, I looked up pitchers of an older generation to see if they were still alive. Happily, Curt Simmons, the mainstay of the 1960s Phillies, was still going; he was my father's age, born in 1929, and my father was still alive as well. The other pitching Dobson of Pat's era, the injury-plagued Chuck Dobson, was still alive at a slightly younger 62. But other research showed that Dobson's death was no fluke. Two of the many players for whom Dobson had been traded at various points in his career, were dead: Johnny Oates (58) and Joe Niekro (61). Dobson had famously been part of the only pitching staff ever to have four twenty-game winners: himself, Dave McNally, Jim Palmer, and Mike Cuellar, all on the 1970 Baltimore Orioles. McNally, a key figure on baseball players winning rights to free agency, had died in 2005, at age 59, of lung cancer (he had always been a heavy smoker), in his beloved Montana. I knew Palmer was still alive. What about Cuellar? Yes! The wily Cuban-American, called "Crazy Horse" during his career, was still alive, in Florida, still active and busy. Like Ringo Starr and Paul McCartney, two of the four twenty-game winners survived.

Why exactly was Dobson so important to me? It is hard to put into words. I was nine years old and just beginning to be immersed in baseball, just vaulting from knowing nothing but the barest aspects of the game to being totally quickened and captivated. The familiarity with which the newspapers referred to "Dobson" fascinated me. A conversation was ongoing and I did not have the right cues to enter it. But others had these cues. How is a young boy to crack the mysterious semiotics of the sports pages? How to weave his way into their mysterious sign-systems? That sense of Dobson's being an assumed part of the sports page narrative intrigued me and spurred me to become familiar with this narrative myself. Within a few months I knew as much about baseball as was possible. In that same interval, Dobson, who had been considered on the edge of journeyman status, became the Yankees' most consistent pitcher down the stretch run—the first I ever witnessed—and ended up winning 19 games and almost pitching the team into the playoffs. Yet loyalties at that age are still dispensable. Dobson had an indifferent season the following year. And I did not weep when he was traded to Cleveland. In fact, looking back one now sees he had a fairly good year for the Indians in 1976, winning sixteen games. But my global assumption at the time was that he was washed up. I see, on the Baseball Reference website, that Dobson, after having had a bad year in 1977, was released by Cleveland on April 14, 1978. I forget exactly what I was thinking on April 14, 1978. But be assured that it was not about Pat Dobson. He had been consigned to an archaic stratum of awareness as remote as any antiquarian residue.

Athletes in a way 'die' when they retire. But the sports fan always knows the retired athlete is alive in a different dimension, still there in a corner of one's perception, still theoretically "available." That he would 'always' be alive, always be there as a reference point, as an object of reverie, as a subject of what Wallace Stevens would call "musing the obscure," was never in perceptual doubt. When our childhood heroes begin to die, we know we are mortal. Moreover, we have the new task of remembering that person's heroism for ourselves and for others. That this hero was a capable, though not extraordinary right-handed pitcher is, in essence, no different than if he were a great writer or musician or statesman. Pat Dobson gave me the wonderful gift of being nobody but himself. Nothing he did was specifically for me. Yet without him my life would not have been what it was.

Part of the world is gone. It is as if furniture in a room of the house which we never visited, but which we still valued, suddenly vanished. After this, we ourselves have to be a larger part of the world than we had been. This is a tough burden. But it is, unavoidably, a necessary one. Growing older can be described as the transition from having people be parts of the world to helping make the world for others. To be a part of other worlds is to be a part of the perceptual horizon against which we live our lives. People have an informational awareness of other people who exist, distantly, likely never to be met personally. Yet these people function as part of the plenitude and richness of one's private world.

Later the same weekend, I read the obituary of Robert Kupperman (71) in the *Times*. Kupperman was an expert on terrorism who worked in Washington. In the mid-1980's, Kupperman had been ubiquitous on television as a commentator on the hostage and hijacking crises in Lebanon and on other terrorism-related issues. By pure happenstance, I had met Kupperman (who was extremely amiable) at a large party in Washington during that period. In this party full of Washington insiders, or those who aspired to that status, I, a complete outsider, was the only one who remotely recognized Kupperman and made a fuss over him. Whether this was an issue of a kind of Washington protocol, everyone else knowing Kupperman and treating his celebrity with a sort of deflationary decorum, or as manifestly seemed the case, those "insiders" genuinely did not know who he was, it left me with a salutary sense of the limitations even of the most widespread sort of fame. I had noticed that Kupperman was not a staple of post-September 11 television analyses and had concluded that he might be ill. In fact he had been suffering from Parkinson's disease since 1990. In his own sphere—admittedly one of more popular consumption—Dobson was never as ubiquitous as

Kupperman had been at his point of flourishing. Furthermore, the fact that he had played with so many teams—Baltimore, San Diego, Detroit, Atlanta, New York, Cleveland—diminished the intensity of obituaries devoted to him in any one city, though the similarly itinerant career of plane-crash victim Cory Lidle (34) had produced a flood of memories from his many teammates in multiple cities. But Dobson's career had been thirty years ago. The institutional memory of the sports desks in various cities had not registered him. The situation is, of course, even worse for academics. Adeline Tintner (90), the noted Henry James scholar, had to have a paid obituary put in the *Times* by her family, but it was so small it escaped the notice of both me and a friend of mine, both avid Tintner fans, who scrupulously read the obituaries. Marcel Tetel (71), the great scholar of Renaissance French literature who taught at Duke University, was given no obituary in the *Times*, and a listing in the Necrology column of *The Chronicle of Higher Education* was only obtained for him after a concerted campaign by respectful admirers on his behalf.

Dobson's death illustrates two of the aspects of growing older: the burden of asking more of the world than it is capable of giving, and the way even vaguely famous people, after they have died, seem to fade in people's memory as compared to those still active. To take this news well requires a sense of asceticism, to say the least. But it also might require a bracing alertness to chilling realities that might be oddly fortifying. As Wallace Stevens put it in his "Farewell to Florida," *To the cold, go on, high ship, go on, plunge on.*

George Dickerson

Badinage for "Pepper"

(for Thomas M. Catterson, in memoriam)

So you've finally gone to seek your severed leg
And end your body's antic quarrel with time.
Terrific! What's left behind? Here. At the still point.
Where the mirthless clowns of midnight
Snicker: "Hoo ha! Hoo ha! Sweet Pepper's dead,
With Eastern metrics dancing in his head."
This is not so fine, my friend...this hapless end.

You know how absence aches....
You knew before you quit
Your walker's intricate pirouette
The recklessness of wish and want...
The cost...the haunt... ("Jig! Jig!" the jongleur said.
From his busted bed.) But to stop short
The syllables of your heart's fierce muttering
So soon is beyond my knack to grieve.

Hey! Let's take a jaunty, jocular leave
And screw the wizard of finality.
We'll have another cigarette. You bet!
And watch the lovely ladies' last late pass,
Then listen for God's gruff guffaw
As you humpety-bump your raggedy ass
Up the steps of heaven. "Hoo haw!"

Paul Casey

Katie Couric Is No Friend of Mine

Time was when turning 50 for a man meant buying a red convertible or taking up with a blonde secretary. Or both. Now, thanks to Katie Couric, that bitch, turning 50 means having a colonoscopy.

In the waiting room, the first thing I noticed was the bathroom. Not down the hall, *but right there in the waiting room*. Just like the friendly hints in the written instructions on colon cleansing, I suspected irony: After drinking the liquid laxative diluted in 12 ounces of fluid, and drinking an additional four eight-ounce glasses of clear fluid, *you will want to stay near a toilet*.

Little wonder that I am also instructed to have some moist towelettes on hand and Desitin for chapping. I remember a boss once saying, "You know what chaps my ass, Casey?" Now I know. Given my gurgling bowels, I decided to be heartened by the nearby facilities.

The elderly gentleman nearest me wore a Ricky Ricardo two-tone shirt, khakis, brand new white sneakers. His close-cropped silver hair and tanned narrow face made him look like a military man, his eyes staring into the distance. When the nurse called his name, he got to his feet in one motion, turned to leave, stopped, pivoted back, leaned down to kiss his woman on the forehead, then marched to meet the medicos.

I've spent my adult life avoiding doctors. Last time I visited a doctor was 10 years ago when I turned 40 and my wife threatened divorce if I didn't submit to a physical. I submitted. A mere decade later and she's nagging me to get another one, and I know exactly where this will lead. A bad bit of business, that's where. Thanks, Katie.

Fucking doctors.

My mother was a willing victim of Western medicine, which excels at treating symptoms but rarely seeks causes. Consequently, on the counter flanking the kitchen sink, my father's quart of Seagram's VO was surrounded by my mother's pill bottles: steroids, painkillers, mood elevators, tincture of opium. My mother had a lot of illness in her life, so she took a lot of medication. Naturally, I developed an aversion to legal drugs, even the over-the-counter stuff. Doctors weren't my favorites either.

Growing up, I thought everybody's mother went into the hospital one or two times per year for one or two weeks. I have early memories of standing outside the Stanford Medical Center and my father pointing up to the window of my mother's room. Me and my brothers and sisters stood there so she could look down on us. It didn't strike me as unusual until I was a teenager and noticed other parents rarely, if ever, went into the hospital.

The doctors couldn't cure her. Her stomach hurt, she couldn't eat, lost weight; then she was hospitalized where they were happy to try out another cure. Drug treatments, surgery, diets, there was always something new to try. Stanford was a teaching hospital, after all. My mother happily agreed to every treatment, though. Eventually, she was diagnosed with Krohn's disease. She lived with that for twenty years until Leukemia got her in the end.

In my late 20s my wife noticed a small extra flap of skin in my armpit.

"It's nothing. Get the scissors."

"You're going to the doctor."

I didn't have a doctor, so I ended up in the urgent care clinic with a young, male physician's assistant, and he decided I needed a finger wave because of a harmless growth *in my armpit*. Later, curled on the couch at home, I attempted to explain my sense of violation. My wife said, "I've birthed your three children, so don't complain to me about doctors poking you."

Philosophic hindsight now allows the possibility that the finger-wave procedure was strictly diagnostic. If not, then fair play to him. I was a handsome buck then. Still, the incident did little to change my opinion of the medical profession.

Many years later my wife grew restive about a marble-sized bulge on my neck. "That has to go. It's freaking me out."

The first doctor reported that it was a fat deposit; insurance would not cover cosmetic surgery.

"Did you tell him about the cancer on *both* sides of your family?" my wife asked.

Actually, I *had* told him and was shocked when, after cursory fingering of my neck bulge, he hustled me out of his office. Thrilled, of course. But a little alarmed, too.

"We're getting a second opinion."

A young surgeon did finally see me and said insurance wasn't a problem. And somehow I got the idea that the surgery was on a par with a trip to the dentist. "Local anaesthetic; he'll flick that thing out with a melon baller," I explained when my wife offered to accompany me. "I'll be fine."

I firmly believed this, too, until the morning of the surgery when the nurse called to make sure I didn't eat anything. "Since 10:00 pm last night, right?"

I cradled the phone to my chest with my chin to free my hands to spread the mustard on the salami sandwich the call interrupted. I replied, "No, nothing." Then ate my sandwich. I didn't see how a salami sandwich could affect anything one way or another.

My next clue that this was more than getting a tooth filled was the puzzled, concerned look on the admitting nurse's face when I answered, "Well, no, I came alone."

She craned her neck to look past me, "There's nobody with you, really?"

I felt lonely when she said it like *that*.

Then the orderly took my book away.

"No," I explained, tightly gripping the novel I happened to be reading at the time, "this is how I relax. It will help me."

He was a young, pasty-faced fellow; he easily yanked the book out of my hands. "Not sterile."

The more awful memory, an icy jet of fear freezes my bowels when I think of it, was the gurney ride: strapped in, flat on my back, fluorescent light fixtures passing overhead, wind playing down the length of my body, rolled and steered by a stranger's hands. For me, a vision of the future—*this is how you will end, right?*

I was given Versed. I remember the anaesthesiologist telling me what a great surgeon was operating on me. Then I was in the recovery room and they started in on somebody accompanying me. "Mr. Casey, you can't drive yourself home. It's illegal."

"My ride is waiting for me outside," I said.

"Outside?"

A Candy Striper rolled me out to the exit. It was raining past the awning, the parking lot streaked with the overhead lights. "Mr. Casey, I don't see a car out there."

She stopped the wheel chair in between the sliding double doors. "Sure," I said, standing, "it's right down there."

"Mr. Casey, please."

My house was less than a mile away; I easily drove home.

Before you get to have a colonoscopy you receive a physical. Avoiding doctors meant I didn't have a doctor, so my wife worked the phones, which is how I ended up with an attractive young female doctor instructing me to bend over the examination table.

At work the next day, Andy Seubert asked me how it all went. I replied, "A beautiful young woman shoved her finger up my ass and told me I was too fat. All in all, not bad."

My name was called. I remembered to kiss my wife—mental tip of the cap to Mr. Ricky Ricardo shirt—and squared up. I was shown to a curtained-off area that contained a chair and bed and was handed a gown. Once I was gowned and on the bed, an IV was started and I was left alone. That's when I noticed activity in the room across from me. When I figured out the gloved, masked woman's task, I remembered my advice to my teenage daughter one evening while we sat on the couch watching Friends. Sarah, who had the cat on her lap, suddenly thrust the animal off of her lap and screamed. I spotted the problem right away, a turd clinging to the fur on the cat's ass. When my daughter returned from putting the cat out, I told her if that happened to me I would kill myself.

That's how I felt when I observed the woman place the black, serpentine cameras into a dishwasher. They could never get the water hot enough, could they? Each soiled camera was delivered in a large, rectangular plastic container, maybe even Tupperware. Did they scrub those fuckers out?

Eventually, they rolled me a few feet from the prep area into the procedure room where I received an ugly surprise when the doctor instructed me to turn on my left side.

"My *left* side?," I asked. Because then I faced the high resolution screen, a 52-inch terrifyingly clear panel that already contained a white spiderweb with thousands of strands that turned out to be a piece of gauze the camera rested on.

The nurse answered for the doctor, "Yes, your left side. Is there a problem?"

Oh, you glib . . . you think you're going to force me to face my inner self when the camera is inserted in me? Fuck that machine. Fine, I turned on my left and *closed my eyes*.

They dripped the Versed into me and I opened my eyes to

visual wonders, like gliding in an airplane over sand dunes sunset pink.

I am fucking beautiful!

The camera hesitated, hovered over a white flat area, lowered to what appeared to be a slight protuberance. A small claw came into view and gnawed on the polyp and a thin stream of blood bisected the white area and for that brief moment I understood religious ecstasy. It was all so lovely and it was in me. I am lovely inside.

After thirty minutes of recovery, I dressed in my street clothes; the nurse ushered me into a consulting room and then went to the waiting area to call my wife in. Once all three of us were seated, the nurse explained that everything looked good, that they did take one small sample but it was nothing to worry about, worse case is that instead of waiting ten years for the next examination, it might be changed to five or three. "But I don't really expect that," she summarized, and was proven correct when the tersely-worded lab results arrived a week later.

In a hurry to flee I walked ahead of my wife, exiting the room and then down the corridor, eyes on the door out of there. Door knob in hand, I looked back and saw my wife standing in front of the consulting room next to ours, head cocked as if trying to hear through the closed door. I couldn't wait. I skipped out.

She caught me on the sidewalk, said, "They're still in there."

Foggy from the Versed, I wanted to go home.

"The older man, the one in the black and tan shirt, the one they called *before* you. When they called his wife I knew it was your turn—but they're still in the little room."

I turned to the parking lot, "Ricky Ricardo?"

She continued, "Early detection, though, leads to extremely high survival rates. What do you think of Katie now?"

I kept silent and followed my wife out to the parking lot. Dull, grey clouds filled the sky. I hoped Mr. Ricky Ricardo shirt lived a long marching life, but Katie Couric was no friend of mine.

Steve Davenport

Millstadt Dead Wagon

Down to Millstadt and all that hell
The bodies come the bodies go
Carrying things from fall to fell

To ashes ashes ring the bell
Dead wagon going coming slow
Down to Millstadt and all that hell

Yellow grease bone chips a smell
A body never wants to know
Carrying things from fall to fell

Who cares what doesn't render well
Until the wind begins to blow
Down to Millstadt and all that hell

Dead wagon's coming to sell
The bodies it picked high and low
Carrying things from fall to fell

I say fuck this villanelle
That can't stop what's got to go
Down to Millstadt and all that hell
Carrying things from fall to fell

Liam Mac Sheóinín

Graying Genius

I published my first fiction in 2000 at the age of 47. It actually received a Pushcart Prize nomination. *Boylandsday(s)*, a chapter of a work in progress, set in a resort hotel along the Jersey Shore (a princedom by the sea, as Vladimir Nabokov would pitch it) back in the twilight of the roaring eighties, involves a failed sexual encounter between a thirty-five-year-old Irish American gangster and a twenty-one-year-old Jewish American Princess. The phallic failure, Brian Jordan, a surprisingly literate ad canvasser/coke dealer, experiences dreaded sexual dysfunction after a perfect day with the lovely Rachel Neal, someone he believes embodies the perception of space and time to his heart, to remember Proust's deuced good definition of romantic love. The chapter is a Menippean satire, and there's not a serious word in it. Yet, always the satirist, I give it a weepy façade. A parody of feelings, if you will. I am fortunate that I had read everything Joyce (avowed parodist) and Pynchon (Menippean satirist) had ever published before starting *Boylansday(s)*. Also fortunate, I had in my late thirties embraced the existentialism of Sartre and only a few years later commenced a study of the two Jacques, Derrida and Lacan. As much as I love language, Derrida showed me that on the precious page, words are the vain gestures of a sonic ghost. After all, a deconstructionist reading of Rex Lear allows one to see the deposed king as being damned for a despicable crime. Deconstructionist Shakespeare, who habitually elevates a so-called fool to the position of sage, has Lear's coxcomb wearer palpably hint at his employer's sordid, inconceivable rendezvous with his daughters:

I have used it, nuncle, ever since thou madest thy daughters mothers.

This particular deconstruction is courtesy of Wallace Gray's brilliant *Homer to Joyce*. Gray, who passed away suddenly in 2001, a greatly esteemed professor at Columbia for decades and contributor to a Dubliner website, was remarkable for his textual insights and deductions. I routinely sent my fellow unabashed Joycean, Professor Gray, drafts of my works and was astonished at the praise he bestowed on them. His deconstructions were uncanny. For example, long before I knew it, he presciently declared that Rachel (ewe) would lead boustrophedonic Brian to the slaughter. Not really that bad, when one realizes slaughter is a sight rhyme of laughter. Professor: *In lumine Tuo videbimus lumen!*

Anthony Burgess theorized, in his last years, that it was an artistic imperative to complete a novel in timely fashion. The idea of lucubration, the kind so evident in the work of Joyce and Pynchon, would contrast with his theory of a writer as tradesman. "He made money. A poet, yes, but an Englishman too," as Deasy, referring to Shakespeare, tells Stephen Dedalus in Chapter Two of *Ulysses*. Who are writers, such as Burgess and John Gardner, seldom achieving artistic greatness in their own works, to give artistic imperatives? *On Moral Fiction*, indeed. Whose morals, John? Yours? Mine?

Burgess's two best novels, *Nothing Like the Sun* and *A Clockwork Orange*, are Joycean novels. *Nothing Like the Sun* is little more than an expansion of Stephen's discourse on Shakespeare in the Scylla and Charybdis episode. It seems Burgess didn't mind lucubration as long as he didn't have to squint his stony Mancunian eyes in the inconstant candlelight. He much preferred to write readerly novels and film scripts. In fact, he even dedicated one of his novels to Burt Lancaster. Burgess also contributed articles and book reviews to every conceivable periodical in multiple languages throughout the world. His great pseudonymous review of one of his own books has become a literary legend.

I wish someone would have reminded "Little Wilson" of Robbe-Grillet's dictum: "The true writer has nothing to say. It's the way he says it." Remember Hamlet's answer to a fishmonger who inquires what the Prince was reading: Words. Words. Words. Words like ataraxia, aponia, apophenia, hyperdulia, hypnagogia, underdarkneath, leucodermic, philopornosophical, scatologicalligrapher, girleen, and tuism abound in my fiction. Admittedly, a jarring interruption of the fictive dream. People can say my work is a joke. They're right. It is, however, a purposeful joke. Still, nobody can say anything about the comely basket of words I have picked. Many of them cherry-picked from the pages of a famous banned book. Nabokov, a brilliant wordsman and woodsman (pursuing winged seraphs through many a *selva oscura*), designates his most famous creation, among other things, a girleen (nothing more than a Joycean Englishing of cailin).

Burgess, in his entertaining story collection *The Devil's Mode*, concocts a meeting between the Bard and Cervantes in Valladolid. Cervantes, Burgess tells us, invented the novel and Shakespeare, the English language. Bloom, Roldy, not Poldy, claims Shakespeare invented the literary human. God of the page, Will S, according to Professor Bloom. In my second published fiction, *Boylansday(s) Continues*, a loving parody of Joyce's Circe, a Don Harold Bloom meets up with Shakespeare in a go-go bar owned by my protagonist, Brian. My Circe—like Joyce's—is a horrificomical pseudoblepsia. In the following scene, Anthony Burgess (Little Wilson) and Don Harold Bloom debate the sexual preferences of Shakespeare (Big Will Shakefork).

LITTLE WILSON
(a glass of gin in his hand)
Will is like all Stratford men, he likes dark ladies and fair boys.

DON HAROLD BLOOM

(*sitting in front of vanity, habited as the Dark Lady of the Sonnets, applying makeup, plucking brows*)

You're wrong, Anthony. Stratford men are all for wenches!

LITTLE WILSON

(*holds up glass*) Sláinte! Sorry, Bloom. Stratford men are all for boys! Bloo me. Blo me. Bli me. Bloo me in second best bed.

Shakefork (Wakish for Shakespeare) in my Circe is little more than the mouthpiece for his ghostbard, Oxford. He also delivers the coup de grâce to Josh ben Joseph—nailed to a cross like a bat to a barn—by sticking a spear into the chiropteran prophet's buttock. In a prior scene, a polypneic Josh ben Joseph masturbates on the cross, without hands like a horse, as messiah or magus, his foreskin is magically restored for the purpose, as Brian's girlfriend Rachel struts naked on the stage. I hear the creecries from the religious right, and answer with the declaration:

Blasphemy is a victimless crime!

Unbelievable as it seems, I was once a devout Irish Catholic. This meant I was constantly under the monitorship of the triumvirate in the sky. Abraham, Martin and John. But in all seriousness, when one casts aside Irish Catholicism it is as if one's mind has been manumitted. Free from the bloody nets, as Joyce described Ireland and Catholicism, does not, however, assure one's soul's ascent heavenward. Atheistic Liam MacSheóinín prefers an unbound mind even if it means his alleged soul will plunge into the stygian muck. Voidward I shall go, like Joyce's bleak incense.

In my most Menippean satirical chapter, published in *The Abiko Annual*, written in mock memoir style, the memoirist, Martin Amis (one of my favorite writers), proposes, "Beyond every bright horizon, there's an Enola Gay flying unannounced."

On the morning of January 13, 2000 an Enola Gay invaded

my airspace. I ended up in the hospital after experiencing what I believed was a heart attack. It turned out to be a hiatal hernia caused by years of untreated GERD. I was also, as one would expect from my excessive adoration of the white demon, sugar, diagnosed with Type 2 diabetes. I have for most of my life been a teetotaler, literally a colapot. Processed sugar is certainly as deadly as *uisce beatha*. As some of you might recall, Joyce breathed last on January 13, 1941. A fact not lost on this essayist. The fact I had refused to honor Joyce by duplicating his death date proves Joyceanism has its limits. More importantly, my novel was a long way from Tipperary and entelechy. I had yet to write the chapter in which Dubya, back in the roaring eighties, buys an eightball from my protagonist in the bathroom of a bar located in the fabled Irish Riviera:

•

Thalatta! Thalatta! Warm sunshine merrying over the winedark sea.

An exurban cowboy bursts through a squeaky stall door, forefinger and thumb compressing his flared nostrils.

"This is Brian, George. The guy Larry and I told you about."

"Nice to meet you, Brian. I'm George W. Bush."

The vice president's son's simian brow corrugated. If you want to give a natural appearance to one of them, a Bush for example, use the fosh of an ape, the eyes of a lizard, the ears of a chimp, the schnoz of a redtail hawk, the smile of a Danish villain, the temples of a rattlesnake, and the neck of a tortoise.

"I need to buy some blow, Brian. Can you help me out, partner?" the vice president's son pleaded, texascombing his rebellious snakeblacklocks.

"I have an eightball in my pocket that you can have free of charge." Jordan smiled uncomfortably, adding: "I'm a loyal Republican."

"Did you hear that, Roberto?" the exurban cowboy cried incredulously, his dusky face oscillating in Bushian fashion. "What a guy! I think it's great you'd do that, Brian, but I insist on paying for it. It's the Republican way, partner."

Look at his eyes: reptilegreen. Any closer and he'd be a monopt. His pupils screaming: Fuck Nancy Reagan and Just Say No in her faux royal Taffy arse!

"All right," Jordan said. "If you insist."

●

I arrived at Dubya's "natural appearance" from an epigraph in Thomas E. Kennedy's great book of essays on the writing craft, *Realism & Other Illusions*:

"If you want to give a natural appearance to an imaginary creature, a dragon for example, use the head of a mastiff or a pointer, the eyes of a cat, the ears of a hedgehog, the snout of a hare, the smile of a lion, the temples of a cock, and the neck of a tortoise."

—Leonardo da Vinci

The magnificent Nabokov provides us a remarkable word, a putative transliteration from Russian, for capturing Dubya and his fellow reptiles: *izmena*—meaning, if you believe the unreliable narrator of *Transparent Things*, a slithering creature. I avail of the Nabokovian con or transliteration throughout my fiction to describe those who seem failing in the area of the neocortex. *Izmena* access their worst nature by overriding the mammalian brain for the older, colder reptilian brain. And I believe, sometimes, the override is manifested in their appearance. Tell me truly, friends, you don't see the lizard in Dubya and Laura? Because there exist dragons among us, I often resort to the previously quoted tuistical instructions of a cenacle depicter of some renown in order to better paint *izmena* like Dubya.

Revnons à nos moutons.

There I was in the cardiac unit of the Community Hospital, trapped in an inextricable web of biotelemetry, fully expective of zippered bag status by the end of the day, yet so strong in my atheism that I refused to twist my lips in prayer. And when it seemed as if my date with Dark Rosaleen McFate—for the moment anyway—had been postponed, nobody heard me shout: Go *raibh maith agat a Íosa! How could I? Ah! The fugition of time changes all. The mere ideation of an everlasting soul—for me at least—remains the second human conceit. A second razor cut to the throat of entity multipliers. It's a godless and soulless universe to this inhabitant. When I die, the world ends. Don't worry, friends. I actually feel better than I have in decades. I could probably go on for minutes, as a lower comedian than I would joke. If there are any lower, that is. So for the moment McFate waits. Of course, one day, as the saying goes, I'll be enclosed in clay; however, I assure you, without anyone singing "Non Nobis* and *Te Deum."* Until then, friends, I will use my graying genius to befuddle and befuckle criticasters and *izmena* alike.

photo by John Campbell

Joseph Millar

Midlife

She's slim and seems distracted, the social worker
who visits my apartment, who wants to know
why my ten-year-old was alone New Year's Eve
when the cops came through the door.

His mother was drunk, I say, and I was up north
with my girlfriend who doesn't want any more kids.
Would she like a cup of tea?
We do have some problems here, I know --
as I forcefeed old newspapers into the trash --
but hopefully nothing too unseemly,
no disarray that can't be explained.

I want to say I've tried
to find another way to live,
away from the electric metal wires
that whisper to me in the afternoons,
the snake dreams that follow after,
uncoiling slowly in my sleep
and the supermarkets where I go unconscious,
humming to myself and staring, minutes at a time,
at the olives and loaves of bread.

There's not much to show for all this:
four rooms, a dented Olds, tattered pictures
of Che Guevara and Muhammed Ali,
the Sixties with their fire and music
scattered like highway cinders. Does the State
offer therapy for aging single fathers?
Is it all right to smoke?
Would she like to step into the back where it's dark
and fuck, standing up amid the laundry?
She smiles vaguely, hands me her card,
says she won't need to return.

Later I think this must be what it is
to get older. My knee hurts getting up
from the couch. Can't work like I used to
and my chest hairs are turning gray.
I'm angry with my son, now quietly asleep,
for needing help with everything: homework,
breakfast, rinsing the shampoo from his hair;
and sad as I gather his small raincoat,
the baseball hat saying Surf's Up,
hang them over a chair and start washing the pot
of day-old spaghetti we ate for dinner.

I listen to Miles with the lights off,
knowing the phone won't ring any more
and too tired to shower. I listen to my breath
leave and return, rain falling
into the cold trackless night,
and the wind in the trees outside
like someone passing.

Billy Collins

Forgetfulness

The name of the author is the first to go
followed obediently by the title, the plot,
the heartbreaking conclusion, the entire novel
which suddenly becomes one you have never read,
never even heard of,

as if, one by one, the memories you used to harbor
decided to retire to the southern hemisphere of the brain,
to a little fishing village where there are no phones.

Long ago you kissed the names of the nine Muses goodbye
and watched the quadratic equation pack its bag,
and even now as you memorize the order of the planets,

something else is slipping away, a state flower perhaps,
the address of an uncle, the capital of Paraguay.

Whatever it is you are struggling to remember,
it is not poised on the tip of your tongue,
not even lurking in some obscure corner of your spleen.

It has floated away down a dark mythological river
whose name begins with an L as far as you can recall,

well on your own way to oblivion where you will join those
who have even forgotten how to swim and how to ride a bicycle.

No wonder you rise in the middle of the night
to look up the date of a famous battle in a book on war.
No wonder the moon in the window seems to have drifted
out of a love poem that you used to know by heart.

James Campbell
Grief

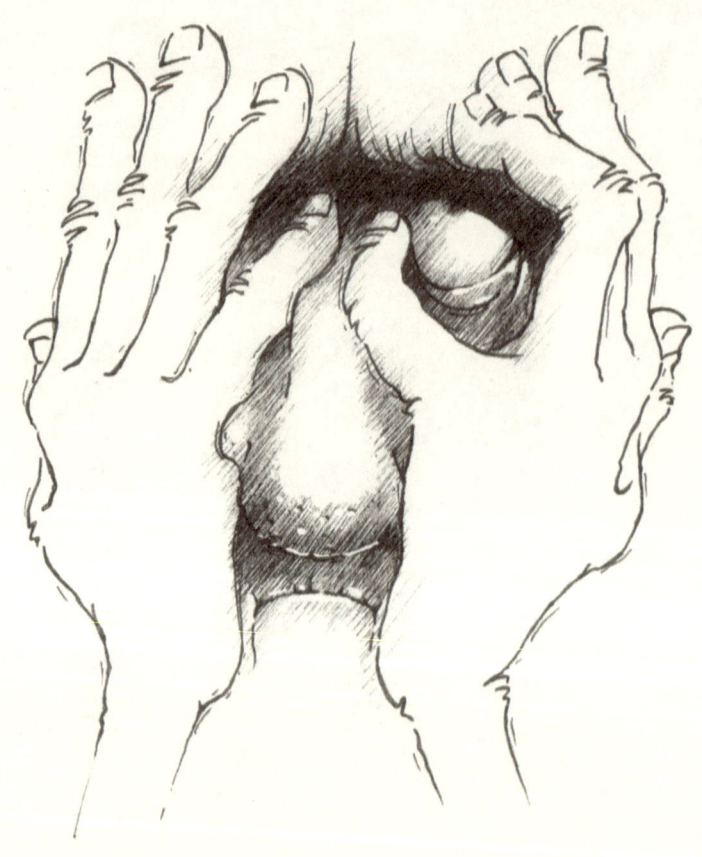

George Dickerson
Toward Absolute Zero

Ambushed by news
That blizzarded the heart...

(Hey, bartender! One more on the rocks,
One more for the frost-heaved road!)

What folklorist foretold a kelpie lurked
Under the mirror of our skating pond—
Cackling with quick-shattering ice?
By a wintry subterfuge,
My boyish wayfarer's feet
Were grabbed, yanked down
In water as frigid as all yesterdays.

Shivering, I clattered out
And crunched toward home—
A foolish kid on awkward stilts
Of pants like frozen boards—
Not finding an enfolding warmth,
But a father's chilly reprimand.

("This old man, he played nine,
He played knick-knack on my spine.")

Down the stone alps to the hospital morgue,
I slid the steep steps of Lord Kelvin's scale,
In the faltering degrees of my dad's demise.

(Hey, Brother, let's piss in the snow!
His carrot nose, his buttons of coal...
These glaciers were once his eyes.)

There on the gurney he froze me out—
A yellowing-purpled lump,
An effigy of cryogenic space
Fleering a fluorescent grimace,
An object that could not have been—
Not father who rode me piggyback,
Whose flushed and sweating cheek
Had ignited my fresh-kindled face—
Not candle wax... nor flesh... not even stone.

I've breathed air as fierce as fire,
When fingers froze to a rifle butt
And cracking ice was a sniper's shot,
In nights so numb they chilled all fear;
But when I kissed that inanimate brow,
I plummeted toward absolute zero
And discovered a loss that seemed to tear
The skin from my fast-stuck lips:
This was a cold too cold to bear.
If matter's mostly motion and motion is heat,
What stops bites the heart with icicle teeth.

You can't warm a father congealed to the core,
Forever a phantom glazed in the mind...
How love a thing that's *no* thing anymore?
Lord, let us forgive! Lord, let us be kind!

Michael S. Begnal

Paul Tillich Never Took Ativan

The German existential theologian Paul Tillich wrote, "The fear of death determines the element of anxiety in every fear. Anxiety, if not modified by fear of an object, anxiety in its nakedness, is always the anxiety of ultimate non-being" (*The Courage to Be*, 1952). In other words, all fear is ultimately the fear of death. And likewise, I think, the fear of aging is also the fear of death. The body begins to break down, health issues start to loom, either for real or as paranoid fears. Every year it's one year closer to death.

Somewhere about age forty, maybe, you are suddenly aware that death is right around the corner. You begin to feel older in the bodily sense. Now there are little twinges, little signs of age. Like some heart palpitations you freak out about — a serious condition or simply stress? After some consideration, it appears to be the latter, but? Oh well, at least you got some Ativans out of it. It's not a life-threatening thing (yet?), but still it is a bit disconcerting to think that there could be anything at all wrong, that the heart is even a consideration, no matter how minor it may (or may not?) be. It's just that tiny realization that you're no longer as immortal as you somehow (now inexplicably) thought you were when you were in your twenties and even into your thirties.

"It is impossible for a finite being to stand naked anxiety for more than a flash of time. People who have experienced these moments...have told of the unimaginable horror of it." Tillich again. The Ativan makes you feel kind of floaty, tired, untalkative. It's better to deal with these thoughts alone. You put aside Nabokov, put on an Iggy Pop solo album, *New Values*, the song "Don't Look Down." Is it coincidence? Isn't it all really this irrational balancing act, in which you somehow stumble forward and try not to worry too much, try to put a lot of shit out of your mind? You've already outlived your father. Another reminder of age, a parent's death, and then your own impending death as people close to you are beginning to fall now. In the vaporous utopia of childhood such a thing would have been unthinkable; now it's here. The horror of it (like Mr. Kurtz: "The horror..."). "It is not the realization of universal transitoriness," wrote Tillich, "not even the experience of the death of others, but the impression of these events on the always latent awareness of our own having to die that produces anxiety." Not the awe that one has as a teenager pondering the "concept" of death, reading books or listening to some music, like when you first get into the Doors (though I still like the Doors). But that deeper "latent awareness" of death which we don't really know is there until it's brought out later by some other experience — how the death of others catalyzes you and interacts with your own dread of your own eventual death.

•

Of the Irish hero Fionn Mac Cumhaill, mythographer/historian Dáithí Ó hÓgáin tells us, "we assume that in archaic Irish lore Fionn had the function of visiting the realm of the dead in order to gain knowledge. This is a shamanic practice which is well-documented among primitive peoples, and Irish tradition itself furnishes much evidence of it. This includes the rituals engaged in by poets, such as composing in the dark and near mounds and raths" (*Fionn Mac*

Cumhaill: Images of a Gaelic Hero, 1988). In this conception, the poet gains a certain power from conversing with the dead. I like to think there's something to this in some way — it appeals to me somehow — though it's probably just as meaningless or meaningful as any other ritual. But my father has appeared in more than a few of my dreams, virtually every one imbued with some weird sense of significance. (This is probably a common thing?) Often he's trying to convey something to me, something important, but which he speaks in obscure language. The setting is usually somehow "the land of the dead," a parallel world which resembles real life in a certain surface manner but is not quite the same. It makes me think of the "Black Lodge" in *Twin Peaks*, or William Burroughs's book of dreams, *My Education*. And here is a poem of my own:

Shade

/BLACK LODGE/
   or like Joyce in Skerries

has gone back to dark his hair and beard
but he is somewhat out of it,
does not speak much at all often,
SIBYLLINE his few words and sentences

or sick and dying pretends health
in a black turtleneck, can of Schaefer,
tossing the can away leaning against my
shoulder,
   "I've been drinking all week,

   it's the only way I feel good"

or like really the first time the lodge
appeared as the living room of house

and there was a vision of the Cross
in cathode light behind my eyelids

spoke of secret children, affairs,
information he had wanted to impart
yet which was also corrupt—I wondered
what way was Persephone's land

   from which no man returns,

heaven or hell or wherever
or my grandmother's old kitchen
in cinder-block public housing,
was cooking a big bunch of bacon (he

spread "jalapeño butter" on first
["It cultures it"], before the frying pan)—
to stand in the kitchen, and to know of women:
"Your whole mood depends on the economy"

   he liked when I said that,

I gave him an old newspaper in the room,
we went downstairs, the little child was with us
like the dream where the child smiles and says   hello,
it was as if it was there all along

but in the carriage weak and frail, and that
"the streets look like they're having sex"
—I put my arm around him—
I knew he was not a hole in the ground

"Joyce in Skerries" refers to Flann O'Brien's novel *The Dalkey Archive* in which James Joyce is discovered not to be dead after all, but living in Skerries, County Dublin, and working as a barman. But he isn't quite all there, is a sort of a shadow of himself.

I remember lying in a dark room at one point, and as I cried seemingly endless tears I thought I could feel the whole fabric of existence rushing through me, like a wind. That really is what it felt like, an intense, visceral wind. It was terrible knowing he was going to die, yet somehow at the same time that wind was a strange affirmation of life. This rush of existence went on for a while, maybe a couple of hours, and the feeling stayed with me for a long period afterward, long after he died. It would strongly resurface when I listened to John Coltrane's *A Love Supreme*, especially the fourth part, "Psalm." It was like breath, really, blowing into me from somewhere behind my neck or head. The same breath, I imagined, that Coltrane is talking about in that movement — and Coltrane *is* talking; his horn phrases the words of the poem which is printed inside the album: "God breathes through us so completely...so gently we hardly feel it..." phrased with his tenor. It's a powerful effect when you realize what's going on. It was just beautiful to listen to; it brought tears to my eyes. It still might.

But the point I wanted to make is that it was such an extreme feeling, something like the deepest love imaginable, this sudden rush of existence (which is the only way I could really describe it). I felt that I was somehow a conduit of that flowing wind, silent breath, and suddenly had this deep awareness that there were things I wanted to do in my life, things I didn't even know. And at the same time, the horrible thing (to suddenly come back to that) was that what was happening was my father was dying, dying. And me too.

"The basic anxiety, the anxiety of a finite being about the threat of non-being, cannot be eliminated. It belongs to existence itself" (Tillich). The conjunction between his impending death and the intensity of it, the visceral realness, produced almost a kind of bittersweet feeling multiplied a thousandfold. But it was not depression. Because the experience was part of life itself. How could I expect to avoid pain, unless I was already dead? I was alive. Another poem I wrote:

The Fluctuations

THE FLUCTUATIONS are real,
they warp you sere & black,
they sear you from the inside,
that part of the body

the FLUCTUATIONS,
a transmigration of soul,
lost genealogies, rocky estuary, the Iron
Language,
rain, a structuring gloom—GONE

the fluctuations/
(running through the trenches)
a torrent in a dark room, breath pouring through,
alone in the room don't know how again

(it's the fluctuations)
the zephyrs in the night,
the curtains blowing in somebody else's window,
the charry dry alleys

death & loss dripping from your eyes,
death & loss seeping from your lungs,
death & loss in your twisted black guts like shit,
in the stark stochastic scald
I remember before all of this, how when other people's

parents died, or a friend, or whoever, how it seemed like you had to walk on eggshells for fear of upsetting people or accidentally creating an awkward moment. But when it was happening to me it wasn't like that at all. A big bunch of people came over after the funeral, some of my closest friends, my brother there too of course, and we all got drunk and had a good time. I had a big bottle of Jameson I'd brought over on the plane from Ireland where I was still living at the time. I actually liked talking about it. I didn't want to avoid the fact that my father had just died, though it wasn't exactly a pleasant death. As terrible as it was, I kept thinking to myself, "What can you do...?"

There was a lot of discussion of Kerouac. Kerouac said nobody knows what's going to happen to any of us in the future except for "the forlorn rags of growing old." He drank himself to death at age 47, ended up coughing blood for a whole day in a hospital, finally dying of hemorrhaging esophageal varices. Twenty-six transfusions didn't help. Not a pleasant way to go either, and not exactly the romantic notion that's conjured up in the phrase "drank himself to death." But most people's deaths are unpleasant. In fact, they usually seem tortuous and excruciating.

I began writing this essay a few years ago, at age 41. I'm 44 now, probably 45 by the time this book is published. But I don't really care about my age. It seems like I have to constantly explain myself to people who stand there, gape-mouthed, apparently in shock, thinking I am 25. Well, whatever about that, I suppose if given the choice I'll take the forlorn rags of growing old over hemorrhaging esophageal varices. Until one or the other of these comes I can't worry about it too much. I guess I'll just keep going as long as I can, put Tillich away for a while, keep writing poems, play loud music, and hope that I'll die painlessly at the age of 88, or later.

Jack Driscoll

Fishing The Backwash

Within the week
a fish will enter my heart.
All my life
he has struggled through this undertow
of blood, struggled
while I waded deep into the mirror, childhood
flashing in my eyes like a lure.
I would stare,
pain floating behind the calm surface
of glass. And sometimes, lifting my arm,
I would cast that distance back
to my crib,
       where at night
I dreamed I was tying a knot on the black dock,
narrow and rocking against the cold.

When I awakened, already fifty,
my hands were tangles of old line, my homemade pole
the memory of a cane
lost in the snow. I bend now
with this broken net, this empty stringer
tied like a noose to my belt.

Mario Vargas Llosa

Diatribe Against the Sportsman

I understand that in summer you surf the rough waves of the Pacific and spend the winters skiing down the Chilean trails at Portillo, the Argentine trails at Bariloche (since the Peruvian Andes do not permit such affectations), that you sweat every morning doing aerobic exercises at the gym, running around athletic tracks or parks or streets, encased in a thermal suit that squeezes your ass and belly like the old-fashioned corsets that asphyxiated our grandmothers, that you never miss a soccer game or the classic encounter between *Alianza Lima* and *Universitario de Deportes* or a boxing match for the South American, Latin American, North American, European, or World title, and that on these occasions, glued to the television set and making the show even more agreeable with beer, *cuba libres*, whiskey on the rocks, you yell at the top of your lungs, turn red in face, howl, wave your arms, or become depressed with every triumph or failure of your idols, as befits a loyal sports fan. More than enough reasons, Señor, to confirm my worst suspicions regarding the world in which we live and to classify you as a brainless, mentally defective shithead. (I use the first and third terms as metaphors; the second is to be taken literally.)

---

*Excerpted from the novel, *The Notebooks of Don Rigoberto*

Yes, it's true, in your atrophied intellect a light has come on: I consider the practice of sports in general, and the cult of sports in particular, as radical forms of the imbecility that brings human beings close to sheep, geese, and ants, three extreme examples of animal gregariousness. Control your wrestler's impulse to tear me to pieces and listen; in a moment we'll talk about the Greeks and the hypocritical *mens sana in corpore sano*. First, I should tell you that the only sports I do not find ridiculous are those of the table (excluding Ping-Pong) and the bed (including, of course, masturbation). As for the rest, contemporary culture has transformed them into obstacles to the development of spirit, sensibility, and imagination (and, consequently, of pleasure). And above all, of consciousness and individual freedom. In our time nothing, not even ideology and religion, has contributed so much to the rise of contemptible mass-man, a robot full of conditioned reflexes, or to the resurrection of the culture of the tattooed primate in a loincloth which lies concealed behind the facade of modernity, as the glorification of physical exercise and games by our society.

Now we can speak of the Greeks, so you won't pester me anymore about Plato and Aristotle. But I warn you, the spectacle of young Athenian boys smearing themselves with oils in the gymnasium before testing their physical dexterity, or hurling the discus and the javelin beneath the pure blue of the Aegean sky, will be of no help to you but will force you deeper into ignominy, you, a buffoon whose muscles have been hardened at the expense of a lowered testosterone level and a plummeting IQ. Only blows to the head with a soccer ball or the punches received in the boxing ring or the mind-numbing turn of the cyclist's wheels and the premature senile dementia (in addition to sexual dysfunction, incontinence, and impotence?) which they tend to provoke can explain the attempt to establish a direct line between the tunicked youths of Plato anointing themselves with resins after their sensual and philosophical physical displays and the drunken hordes roaring in the stands of modern stadiums (before setting them on fire) at contemporary soccer games, in which twenty-two clowns, depersonalized by garishly colored uniforms and running wildly after a ball on a grassy rectangle, serve as the pretext for exhibitions of collective insanity.

In Plato's day, sport was a means, not the end it has become in these municipalized times. It served to enrich human pleasure (masculine pleasure, since women did not engage in sports), stimulating and prolonging it with the representation of a beautiful, smooth, oiled, well-proportioned, harmonious body, inciting it with pre-erotic calisthenics and certain movements, postures, frictions, bodily exhibitions, exercises, dances, touches, inflaming desire until participants and spectators were catapulted into coupling. That these encounters were eminently homosexual neither adds to nor subtracts from my argument, nor does the fact that in the sexual realm Yours Truly is boringly orthodox and loves only women—indeed, only one woman—and is totally disinterested in active or passive pederasty. Understand me, I have no objections at all to what gays do. I am delighted that they enjoy themselves, and I support their campaigns against discriminatory laws. Beyond that I cannot go, for very practical reasons. Nothing related to what Quevedo called the "eye of the ass" gives me pleasure. Nature, or God, if He exists and wastes His time on these matters, has made that concealed aperture the most sensitive of all the orifices that pierce my body. Suppositories wound it, and the tip of the enema syringe makes it bleed (once, during a period of stubborn constipation, one was forced into me, and it was terrible), and so the idea that certain bipeds enjoy having a virile member inserted there fills me with horrified amazement. I am certain, in my case, that along with howls and screams, I would experience a true psychosomatic cataclysm if that aforementioned opening were to be penetrated by an erect penis, even if it were a Pygmy's. The only punch I ever threw in my life was aimed at a physician who, without warning and on the pretext of determining if I had appendicitis, attempted to commit upon my person a form of torture disguised by the scientific label "rectal examination." Despite this, I am theoretically in favor of human beings making love inside out, upside down, alone or in couples or in promiscuous collective (ugh!) matings in which men copulate with men, and women with women, and both with ducks, dogs, watermelons, bananas, cantaloupes, and every imaginable disgusting thing if it makes them agreeable to the pursuit of pleasure, not reproduction, an accident of sex which one must accept as a minor inconvenience but in no way sanctify as the justification for carnal joy (this imbecility on the part of the Church exasperates me as much as a basketball game). But I digress: the image of aging Hellenes, wise philosophers, august legislators, battle-scarred generals, or high priests frequenting gymnasiums in order to revive their libidos with the sight of youthful discus throwers, wrestlers, marathon runners, or javelin hurlers—that image moves me. The kind of sport that panders to desire I condone and would not hesitate to engage in if my health, age, sense of the ridiculous, and leisure time were to permit it.

There is another instance, even further removed from our cultural environment (I don't know why I include you in this fraternity since, as a result of soccer's kicks and blows to the head, cycling's sweaty exertions, karate's throws to the ground, you have been excluded from it), when sport also has an excuse. And that is when a human being, by engaging in it, transcends his animal nature, touches the sacred, and rises to a plane of intense spirituality. If you insist on our using the dangerous word "mystic," then so be it. Obviously such cases, by this time extremely rare—an exotic reminiscence is the warlike sacrifice of the Japanese sumo wrestler, fed from childhood on a fierce vegetarian diet that elephantizes him and condemns him to die, his heart bursting, before the age of forty, and to spend his life trying not to be expelled by another mountain of flesh exactly like him from the small magic circle to which his life is confined—cannot be compared to those idols of the mob that post-industrial society calls "martyrs to sport." Where is the heroism in being turned to mush at the wheel of a racing car propelled by motors that do all the work for humans, in regressing from a thinking being to a mental defective with brains and testicles mangled by the practice of intercepting goals or striving to achieve them just so that maddened crowds can be desexed by ejaculations of collective egoism at each point scored? For contemporary man, the physical exercises and skills called sports bring him no closer to the sacred and the religious; they distance him from the spirit, and brutalize him by catering to his most ignoble instincts: tribalism, machismo, the will to dominate, the dissolution of the individual ego in an amorphous gregariousness.

I know of no lie more base than the phrase taught to children: "A sound mind in a sound body." Whoever said that a *sound mind* is desirable? In this case, "sound" means stupid, conventional, unimaginative, and unmischievous, the vulgar stereotype of established morality and official religion. Is that a "sound" mind? It is the mind of a conformist, a pious old woman, a notary, an insurance salesman, an altar boy, a virgin, a Boy Scout. That is not health, it is an impairment. A rich, independent mental life demands curiosity, mischief, fantasy, and unsatisfied desires, which is to say a "dirty" mind, evil thoughts, and the blossoming of forbidden images and appetites that stimulate exploration of the unknown, renovation of the known, and systematic disrespect toward received ideas, common knowledge, and current values.

Furthermore, it is not even true that engaging in sports in our day creates sound minds in the banal sense of the word. Just the opposite occurs, and you know that better than anyone, for in order to win the hundred-meter dash on Sunday you would put arsenic and cyanide in your competitor's soup, swallow every vegetable, chemical, or magical drug to guarantee your victory, corrupt or blackmail the judges, devise medical or legal schemes to disqualify your rivals, and live hounded by your neurotic fixation on the victory, the record, the medal, the dais; this has turned you, the professional sportsman, into an artificial creation of the media, an antisocial, nervous, hysterical psychopath, the polar opposite of that sociable, generous, altruistic, "healthy" individual to which imbeciles wish to allude when they still dare to use the expression "sportsmanship" in the sense of a noble athlete filled with civic virtues, when, in fact, what lurks behind the phrase is a potential assassin willing to kill referees, murder all the fans of the other team, devastate the stadiums and cities that house them, and bring about the final apocalypse, not for the high artistic purpose that led to the burning of Rome by the poet Nero, but so that his club can win a fake silver cup or he can see his eleven idols carried to a rostrum, flagrantly ridiculous in their shorts and striped undershirts, their hands to their chests and their eyes shining as they sing the national anthem!

(Translated from Spanish by Edith Grossman)

Duff Brenna

A Way with Cows

For three days snow has gathered in a wide band across northern Wisconsin, piling four feet high in some places. My farm is ten miles south of Lake Superior. This area often gets what is called "lake effect snows." Which means two to three feet more than what Hayward, Spooner or Rice Lake get. The skies are clearing, the temperature falling. The wind blows harder. The quiet cocooning effect of lazily falling snow has vanished. The last time I looked at the thermometer it was touching thirty below. Wind-chill fifty below. Grease in axles has crystallized. Oil in oil pans thick as tar. I have thirty-eight cows to care for. Six calves. Numerous cats. I am forty-one years old and have only farmed for two years. I am barely getting by on my once a month milk check.

The farm is old. The barn is leaning, its sloping roof struggling under tons of snow. Wind playing with the top layer, swirling it, gives the effect of a dancing shroud. Every time I go to the loft, I can hear tamarack creaking, complaining. For seventy-five years the old barn has stood against all weather, but I'm wondering how much more it can handle. There are thin snorts of freezing air coming through warped gaps in the walls. Tiny drifts of snow piling up here and there on the hay in the loft. All the tie beams and king posts are frosted. All the rafters curve inward, forming shallow basins threatening to crack and let the snow sift in.

When I finish throwing down hay from the loft, I go to the parlor and feed the cows and calves. Then I check on Minna, who is in labor, and find the tendons soft at the base of her spine. Swollen vulva drooling. Gluey fluids hang like taffy. When the pains hit her, she does a little hoof-to-hoof dance, a two-step sort of. The stanchion rattles. She swishes her tail as if trying to swat the pain.

"Be a big girl," I tell her. My head aches from tension and worry and lack of sleep. There is a tic in my right eyebrow driving me crazy. I rub my eyes with the heels of my hands and only succeed in making things worse. I might be getting another migraine. There is a vague numbness on the right side of my face again. Right hand feeling oddly weak, a symptom experienced by my grandfather when he had a stroke—the numbness, weakness on one side. Two days later he was dead.

"You're too young to have a stroke," I say.

Well, maybe not too young. Forty-one, but I feel sixty and decrepit. I'm lean and wiry, but fifteen pounds underweight—150—and have not been well lately. I feel the undertow of high blood pressure, ulcers, frail nerves, fear of failure tugging at my backbone. I think about San Diego, where I was a part-time lecturer at San Diego State and worked nights in a shipyard, running a gantry, putting tons of steel in place that would one day slip down the ways as an oil tanker or a ship for the navy. I don't want to go back there to southern California—too many people, too many houses jammed together, too much brutal traffic. Ugly brown hills in summer. Heat. Road rage. I was raised in Minnesota and Colorado. I crave green summers. I love autumn, but not winter. I thought I would love winter because it would give me time to write, but that was a pipe dream, that was pie in the sky. I sold everything to buy a farm in Wisconsin (couldn't afford Minnesota). Now I have 140 acres and cattle to care for. I am in debt up to and beyond my ears. I had the mistaken idea that I would sit upstairs in my study finishing the novel I was writing, a semi-biographical story about a farm girl named Mamie Beaver, she who had extraordinary strength and was an idiot savant as well, and probably autistic. A fifteen-year-old farm boy fell in love with her when she was twenty. I wanted to stare at white fields and be inspired to write their story, but truth is I am usually too tired to write. I work on poetry now and then, bits of it scrawled on scraps of paper I keep in my pockets.

The farm and the dreams are fading, but what am I supposed to do? Give up? Go back to teaching? I don't want to teach anymore. Go back to running heavy equipment? I'd rather not. For all its hardships, I love dairy farming. I love the cows, the land, the summer haying, the October beauty of the woods. I love the independence. The isolation. The July evenings when twilight doesn't fail until after ten. And the only sounds are the sounds of nature getting ready for bed. Breezes sighing through the trees alongside the house. The stream twenty yards away burbling the same pacifying verse. Small rewards that add up to big reasons for staying. For risking everything at my foolish age.

Minna shifts hard against my shoulder. The movement saying, *Do something!*

I rub the base of her spine to calm her down. "I'm here," I say. "Everything will be all right. Don't worry."

And I tell her how great she is. Best cow in the barn. When she freshens she'll do a hundred pounds a day, and I will make sure she gets everything she needs. I have been to Fleet & Farm and bought Kow Kare, full of Vitamins A, D and E. There is liquid calcium standing by in case she goes down with milk fever. For respiratory problems, or if her calf gets scours, I have antibiotics.

All the contingencies are covered, I tell myself. Nothing can happen that I can't handle. The pain in my head increases, so I go to the milkhouse, to the medicine cabinet, and grab the bottle of Bufferin and take three with milk from the bulktank. And I think: What if it stays so cold the tractor won't start again today? What if the electricity goes off once more? It was off ten hours yesterday.

What if?

After I feed the cows, I put more straw under Minna in case she wants to lie down. Again she dances the two-step. When the contractions subside she goes back to inhaling hay as fast as she can. It is one of the things I have noticed over the years—the way cows will eat ravenously when they are distressed. Fear is gluttonous. Minna turns her head and looks at me, her nostrils flaring. A sheaf of hay in her jaw, working like a mower's cut-bar side to side. Her rough tongue shattering leaves. Her eyes are huge and rolling, showing startled whites.

"My coo, my honey," I sing, rubbing her backbone, rubbing her flanks.

I leave Minna and turn on the air-compressor, bring out the De Laval milk machines. It is six in the morning. I worry that my headaches and exhaustion may be symptoms of something serious. Or am I just too old to be doing this? Who starts dairy farming at forty? What fool would do that? I have no insurance and there is no money for doctors.

I rub a frosted window with my sleeve and see a diffused light over the southeast horizon, the fields stretching to the forty acres of woods that I own. The trees are naked against the morning sky. Branches reaching like frozen beggars. All over Wisconsin cows and farmers are waiting anxiously for this Arctic bubble to pass.

Moving the milkers, I slip the inflations on the teats of the next cow and feel an electric tingle in my hands. My palms are peeling. Dead dots of skin beg to be bitten. I nibble my palms, bite my fingernails. The lungs of the milkers breathe and the exhaust fans whir. The barn smells of hay, warm cow, methane.

Again I look out the window at the fields faintly blue in the swelling light and I wonder what if some limb cracks and brings the lines down? What if the rafters give way and the snow comes in and drowns the hay in the loft? What if I run out of propane? What if the cold lasts another week? Or two? People die this way and no one knows it until the mailman sees their mail piling up. But the snow on the roads can't last forever. Surely the plows will be out today or tomorrow. The roads will be opened in two or three days at the most. Won't they? I've got cans of soup in the pantry. I've got cereal. Lord knows I've got milk.

Shifting a milk machine to Curious, I recall when she was off her feed last year and her production fell to hardly more than a quart a day. There was no apparent reason for her condition, and my mind turned over images like Taro cards for cows: mastitis thick with garget, full of white cells and fever, hard quarter feverish. Metal disease? A tiny wire gouging her stomach? Which one? First? Second? All four, maybe? Or maybe hoof rot, woody tongue, Johne's disease, a torsion? It was one of the few times I have had to call the vet in. He came out and diagnosed a displaced abomasum. Together the vet and I rolled her, trying to release the gas and get things back in place. But it didn't work, and finally there was nothing to do but cut her open. "Cut her or ship her," is what he said.

It was going to cost too much, but I gave him permission and watched him operate, watched him give Curious just enough anesthetic to numb her nerves but keep her standing in her stall. His scalpel cut a great gash in her hide, scarlet meat and dull white fat. The wound almost bloodless. "Shall I cut you a steak?" he asked, grinning. The incision was shaped like a giant vagina through which a micro-fog was exhaling. The fog reeking of wet organs hungry for life. The vet released the gas from her floating stomach and tied it down. Stitches hung like spider legs from the bottom of her belly. More stitches climbed up her side. Dopey-eyed and listlessly chewing cud, she was unaware of what the vet had done. And now, a year later, she has had a calf and milks well enough to earn her keep. There is nothing but the faintest scar to remind me of how she cheated death. That's the thing I know about cows now. Given half a chance they will pull through. They are so tough so resilient, my bovinities.

It was Wes Johnson who told me that I loved my cows too much. He said I shouldn't give them names, only numbers. "You gotta grow calluses on your heart if you're going to last," he said. That was the day the cow named Jewel was down with sciatic nerve damage after giving birth. I had driven the tractor over to the Johnson farm to borrow a bottle of calcium because I thought Jewel had milk fever. Wes came back with me and we dripped the calcium into Jewel's carotid artery. Then tried to get her up. She couldn't get up no matter how we pushed and prodded. Her right hind-leg pawed helplessly, like a dog wanting to shake hands, and I told Wes it was her sciatic nerve. He agreed. We put the iron O rings around her hips and hooked the rings to a chain-fall hanging from a beam in the ceiling. I cranked Jewel to her feet. "She stands or she's dead," Wes told me. "That's the rule for dairymen."

She stood with the help of the cowlift. But she was very unsteady. She stared at me with expectation and wonder, but I could do nothing except rub the base of her spine and tell her everything would be okay. Her rear end listed starboard, her sciatic leg continually jabbing the air. I massaged the thigh and hip, digging for their chemic cores, hoping to make the blood flow warm with healing power. But it did no good. "Naw, I've seen this too many times," Wes said. "She'll cost money and have to be slaughtered anyway. When you get this sort of thing, it's best to shoot her. What we need to do is get her to the door, get her outside, where we can shoot her and hook her to the tractor and haul her out of the barnyard. Might as well get it over with. Times like this a farmer's got to show no mercy, Duff."

I said we should give her more of a chance. Give her a week. But he said it was hopeless. She wouldn't be paying her way. He knew that I was barely breaking even. Feeding a cow that couldn't produce was self-defeating. He had cranked her down by then and released her from the stanchion and together we pushed and pulled and tried to scoot her towards the door, but she was too heavy. Then

Wes used an electric prod, shocking her. She flopped forward on her side, like a seal. The prod zapping her hips and spine, blue flames leaping from her hide. Desperately she tried to rise, her legs flapping, bouncing her thousand pounds along the concrete floor. I could see she wasn't going to make it. I called a halt. I told Wes no more shocks. Let's shoot her where she lies and we can snake a rope around and pull her out. I went in the house and got my rifle. When I got back I knelt beside her. Resting her anvil head against my thigh, she relaxed as I stroked her. Her eyes closing. And, angry with myself, I covered my face and wept. And Wes said, "What did I tell you? You gotta grow calluses if you're going to last." "I'm not shooting her," I told him. "Let's get her back in her stall."

"Jesus, Duff, you really don't belong here."

I was new to farming then and didn't know how resilient cows could be. But I was convinced I shouldn't listen to Wes too quick with the trigger. I can shoot or ship a cow if forced to, but from Jewel on, I have always given the sick ones every chance. And most of the time they've come back. Jewel healed. One evening a month after her leg failed her, I went to make my last rounds before going to bed, and there she was standing on her own, the right hip scarred by the cowlift, but strong enough to support her. I started laughing. I shouted her name and pounded her rump. She looked at me as if I were crazy. She got strong again. She stood in line in her stanchion to get milked. Cows do that—they surprise you. For a while anyway. For a while, just like old and ailing humans, the inevitable might be postponed. If cared for properly, most dairy cows will average five to six years or more of production before going to Packerland.

Curious flicks her tail over my arm. "You gals are lucky to have me," I say. "I'm a sucker, that's what I am." Curious shakes her head. —No you're not, she says. You need us! And, of course, she is absolutely right.

When the milking is over, I turn my attention back to Minna. Her water has broken and the birthing sack, a gray-pink membrane, is tapping at her heels. She has quit trying to get the baby out. Her muzzle is buried in the hay trough.

"This ain't good," I tell her. My head starts throbbing again. The nerves along my spine twitter as they always do when I think that something might be too much to handle. Standing behind Minna, I tell myself that this is it. I can't take anymore. Life is too hard. I'm so goddamn old and tired. Running a dairy farm is a constant war. Well, maybe not. There are good times too, but this is one of the bad times. "This is one of those moments of truth," I say aloud. "And I need help."

Pacing the aisle, I keep thinking of Cristobell in the cold woods and working like a man possessed to pull her calf out. That baby was backwards. And after two or three hours I managed to get its hind legs up and into the steaming air. The rest was fairly simple. So I need to put my hand in Minna and find out if history is repeating itself.

Stripping off chore jacket, shirt, undershirt, I go to the sink in the milkhouse, scrub my right arm with soap and hot water. I go back to Minna, leaving my hand slippery with suds.

My hand slips down a tunnel warm and easy and comes quickly to a formless mass of hair, muscle and bone. As I move my fingers around, I make out the boundary of a shoulder. Twisted backwards behind it is the calf's neck and head. The baby is bent like a horseshoe. It's about as bad as it can be. I have never had to deal with anything so complicated. I could get the vet to come out when the road is cleared, but that would probably be too late. And where would I get the money to pay him, anyway? For six months I've been in the hole and living on bank loans. I need Minna's milk. I need Friendly and Big Mama and Beth to freshen too. They are all due.

Minna stares at me, her eyes bulging with questions. "I know, I know," I say.

—Get it out of me!

"It's jammed, Minna. I might have to cut it up and take it out in pieces. I've never done that before. I don't really know how to. I might cut you up inside. This is awful. Maybe I better just call the vet and pray he can make it in time."

I look around as if someone is there to tell me what to do. I could call Wes. No, not him. He'd end up killing Minna for sure. There's Tom T or Ed Liska, but I am scared of what any of them might do. Farmers can't afford to mess around with stricken cows. There is nothing for it but to force the issue. If I don't, Minna will die and so will her baby. At least if she dies it won't be because I didn't try everything I could to save her.

Slipping inside her again, I force my fingers between the wedged neck and the womb wall. I try to push the baby forward, but nothing moves. I want to get my fingers in the nostrils and use them to pull the head around. But I can't. Then Minna starts another contraction. She tightens her stomach and bears down. It feels like I'm in a vise, someone turning the handle harder, crushing my hand. The blood feels ready to burst through the tips of my fingers.

"You're making things worse!" I yell. I struggle, cuss, groan until my strength and tolerance for pain wears out. I give up. I pull out. I turn in a circle, whipping my pulsating hand.

There is blood in the sack flowing from Minna. Blood covers my hand and arm. Maybe I've ruptured something inside her? I shake that thought from my mind and focus on how to get the calf unwound. And that's when I see the herding stick. It's the one I use to herd the cows, to tap them along when they're out in the pasture. It's in the corner next to the door. I pick it up and snap it over my knee. At both ends of a six-inch piece I tie baling twine. Then I force the stick, like a horse's bit, into Minna's mouth. I pull the twine over her head and use the other part of the stick, like the handle of an auger, twisting the twine behind her ears. Using more twine, I tie the stick to her neck. It's an old trick that Liska told me about. The pressure pulling on the cow's mouth will often lessen the force she uses bearing down. Minna doesn't like it at all. She shakes her head, her ears sounding like wooden clappers.

Again my hand goes inside and feels the baby. I am able to push it forward slightly. I can almost get my hand around and slide it along the curve of the neck. "It's working," I tell her. "I can feel its ear! I got its ear in my hand!"

But the shaking of Minna's head causes the stick to work loose and the bit to fall out. The next thing I know she is crushing my fingers again. I retreat once more and yell at her, telling her to be still. Doesn't she know I'm trying to help her? "Stupid cow! Quit shaking!" She hangs her head. She snuffs hay.

Walking to the far end of the barn, I look out the window at the fields of snow. Such a long winter. So much intense cold. "Deal with it. Deal with it." That's what my grandfather, a farmer all his life, would tell me if he were alive.

As if sensing the turmoil within the barn, a coyote howls. I've heard that sound for months, the howl coming from somewhere around the southern curve, where the land plunges into the woods. I think of the coyote that followed the haybine last summer catching mice. And I wonder if the howl is hers. Sun spills over the windowsill and brightens the glass. I hear Minna shift again. — Come here! she commands.

I go back to the wooden bit, slip it in her mouth and tie it so tightly to her neck I'm afraid I might choke her.

Grabbing a two-foot piece of baling twine, I cinch one end around my hand and once more enter Minna. With the twine looped between two probing fingers, I place the heel of my hand against the calf's shoulder and push it as hard as I can. It shifts forward and gives me some wiggle room. Minna is busy fighting the bit in her mouth.

Wedging my fingers between the canal and the calf's neck I slip them down a narrow passage. And then I feel the ear again.

Then an eye. The nose, the nostrils. I slip the noose around the nose and tighten it.

"Got it."

I push the calf forward, while my outside hand pulls the baling twine. Push and pull, push and pull, and slowly the head eases around. And finally faces the way out. Going back in with the twine and slipping the noose around the hooves I push and pull some more and ease the legs upward. I can see the hooves now, two yellow-white wedges. I pull them into the light.

"Let go now," I say, untying the wooden bit. "I want you to bear down now. Bear down hard, Minna!"

As I pull on the little hooves, Minna does what I tell her and the calf slides through and into my arms, soaking me with warm birthing fluid.

The calf is dead. Opening the legs I see I have a male. Now it's coyote food.

Laying the dead calf in the aisle, I tell myself that at least Minna is still alive.

"The calving is done," I tell her. "It's over, Minna."

But even as I stand there panting and wishing I could take a bath and go to bed, I see a bubble pushing out of Minna's vagina. The bubble is purple. It gets bigger and bigger. Inside it I see a pair of hooves. "I got another, I got twins," I say. "No wonder it was so jammed up in there! Minna, what're you doing, girl? Supercow or what?" Breaking the sack, I grab the hooves and soon another baby is soaking in my arms.

This one is a heifer. She's alive. There's a starburst on her forehead and her belly is white. The rest of her is black. "Get a load of you!" I say, rubbing the heifer with straw. I carry her around to the manger and set her in front of Minna, who gives the baby a good tongue-lashing, stimulating her blood. The other cows strain in their stanchions, nostrils flaring, smelling the calf and wanting to lick her.

"You've got thirty-seven aunts," I say, feeling hopeful, even a little optimistic.

In a while the baby is up, staggering cow-to-cow, getting sniffed, snorted at, and properly licked. She blinks at a brand new world. —Where am I?

•

When their winter confinement is over, the herd is let out of the barn. Some of the younger ones go nuts and run like overgrown children back and forth over the pasture. They bawl. They butt each other. They kick up their heels. A few of them, as if by magic turned into bulls, mount their sisters. The older cows keep their dignity, moving away and browsing new tufts of grass.

Along the pasture's southern peninsula, the trees are thickening with leaves. In the afternoon the herd gathers in the shade of those leaves to sleep, chew cud, stare lazily into space. The dawdling wind is soothing. We'll live forever like this, won't we? the cows always ask me.

My little farm still has its crisis every other day or so—one thing or another breaking down, this or that cow getting sick, a calf with pneumonia, bills coming in that I can't pay. But it isn't anything that breaks me yet.

At this point in time I am unaware how right Wes Johnson is. I don't belong in farming. By May of next year, 1984, the farm will go under and everything will be auctioned off—the cows, machinery, furniture—and in the freedom of defeat I will leave Wisconsin for what will happen over the next few years. Things will fall apart. The center will not hold. And eventually, I will travel many roads, a world of wandering—state-to-state, city-to-city, job after job—until one day I will find myself in southern California teaching again, and working on my novel. I'll be hating the dead, dry hills, the heat, the traffic. I'll be hating the fact that I'm getting too old to be a novelist or get a full-time position, with tenure track, medical and retirement benefits. My lost farm will give a hard birth to *The Book of Mamie*, which I will send out dozens of times to dozens of agents and publishers and be dismissed with form letter rejections for over two years.

But then in my 46th year I will get a phone call from Toby Olson and Andrea Barrett telling me that I have won the AWP Best Novel Award. The University of Iowa will publish it. Soon I'll have an agent, an editor, and a publishing house for my second novel.

Mamie is a book that wouldn't have happened if I hadn't been a dairy farmer and written about cows and the good and the bad of loving them and the land I once owned. So, maybe it was worth it? Or maybe not. How do you measure these things? Five novels later, I continue to write and it's as hard as ever to get published, which is why I'm still teaching on a part-time basis. Writers, don't quit your day job.

Had I been successful and stayed on the farm it would be twenty-two years now. And I've often wondered what if—what if my blood pressure, the migraines, the ulcers and the ceaseless work *had* killed me? And I was nurturing the grass covering a plot in a Wisconsin cemetery? What might then have been said about my time as a dairyman? Impossible question. But it's not impossible to know what I would want engraved on my headstone. Carved in granite below my name and dates, in simple scroll, I would like my epitaph to say: HERE LIES DUFF BRENNA. HE HAD A WAY WITH COWS.

James Campbell

RIP

Jack Driscoll
Elegy: Charles Atlas
(1893-1972)

When you died
I remembered myself at fifteen, posing
half naked in the bathroom mirror,
that skinny kid whose body reeked of loneliness.

I never ordered the barbells, the nutrition tips,
never sent you that snapshot my father took of me
beside the public swimming pool, arms crossed and
      shivering.
But some nights I'd open a superhero comic book
to the back page, try to imagine
how you hauled that locomotive
a hundred yards down those shiny rails,
and how a draft horse strapped later
into that same harness strained and strained
collapsing finally to its knees to die.

Your heart exploded at seventy-nine.
Weakened by the news
I fell asleep on my son's weight-bench
in our basement. He does not know your name,
though in a nap-dream that afternoon

I saw someone who looks like him
screaming for help, unable
to lift that terrible pain from your chest.

So much for your faith in the flesh,
those decades of bulking up
after that Coney Island lifeguard kicked sand
into your face. Atlas,
I do not believe any god ever hoisted the world
the way you did the back end of a Chevrolet in 1941.
That was enough,
nearly the impossible as we saw it,
that bunch who one day grabbed a bumper together,
each of us flexing, expanding our chests

as if we might call you,
the only witness to our grunts and moans,
the enormity of our growing up.

Niels Hav

Encouragement

Isn't it an uplifting thought
that in a few decades we
and this whole confused epoch
with its cynical presidents,
wornout arguments,
mawkish TV hosts, dim journalists,
and the crapitalistic jubilant choir
will be gone?   For all time!
We will disappear.
They will disappear.
I will disappear.
You will disappear.
It will all disappear.
Hurrah!

(Translated from Danish by Per K. Brask & Patrick Friesen)

Biographies

Contributors are listed in the order in which their work appears in the book.

Norman Mailer was the author of more than 30 books. His fiction has won a National Book Award and 2 Pulitzer Prizes. 2007 saw the release of Mailer's final novel, *The Castle in the Forest*. Mailer's interviewer, **Michael Lee**, was the Literary Editor of *The Cape Cod Voice*, and is a member of the National Book Critics Circle. His collection of short stories, *Paradise Dance,* was published in 2002. In 2007 Lee's collection of essays, *In an Elevator with Brigitte Bardot*, was published by Wordcraft of Oregon.

James Campbell graduated in graphic design in what is now called the University of Ulster in the summer of 1969. He went to work for Ireland's now legendary Kinney/Dobson Design Associates gaining experience in all fields of design from huge mosaics to graphics for the BBC. Campbell went on to work for the *Belfast Telegraph* as a visualizer/illustrator and has been working now as a freelance illustrator for the last ten years.

Robert Pinsky is the author of many books of poetry, most recently *Selected Poems (Farrar, Straus & Giroux, 2011)*. *The Figured Wheel: New and Collected Poems 1966-1996*, won the 1997 Lenore Marshall Poetry Prize. His honors include the William Carlos Williams Award, the PEN Volcker Award and the Los Angeles Times Book Award for his translation of *The Inferno* by Dante. During his unprecedented three terms as United States Poet Laureate, he founded the Favorite Poem Project (www. favoritepoem.org).

Gordon Weaver is the author of four novels and 10 short story collections. He has won two National Endowment for the Arts Fellowships, the O. Henry First Prize, and the St. Lawrence Award for Fiction. *Cadence*, the 1991 movie starring Martin and Charlie Sheen, is based on Weaver's novel, *Count a Lonely Cadence*.

James Brown is the author of *The Los Angeles Diaries: A Memoir* (HarperCollins), which was chosen for Best Books of the Year 2004 by the *San Francisco Chronicle, Publishers Weekly,* and *The Independent* in the U.K. His work has appeared in *GQ,*

The New York Times Magazine; an essay in the *Los Angeles Times Magazine*, was also selected for Best American Sportswriting of 2007 (Houghton Mifflin). Brown has written several novels including *Lucky Town* and *Final Performance*. He has received the Nelson Algren Award for Short Fiction, a National Endowment for the Arts Fellowship in fiction writing and a Chesterfield Film Writing Fellowship from Universal/Amblin Entertainment. In 2011 Counterpoint published Brown's latest memoir, *This River*.

Billy Collins is the author of several books of poetry, including *She Was Just Seventeen* (2006) and *The Trouble With Poetry* (2005). From 2001 through 2003 Collins was United States Poet Laureate and Consultant in Poetry to the Library of Congress. He is Distinguished Professor of English at Lehman College, City University of New York, where he has taught for the past 30 years. He is also a Distinguished Fellow of the Winter Park Institute at Rollins College and served as a Literary Lion of the New York Public Library. His latest collection is *Horoscopes for the Dead*.

Thomas E. Kennedy's 25 plus books include the four novels of the Copenhagen Quartet—most recently, *In the Company of Angels* (Bloomsbury, 2010) and *Falling Sideways* (Bloomsbury 2011)—and a novel-in-essays *Last Night My Bed a Boat of Whiskey Going Down* (New American Press (2010). His stories, essays, and translations appear regularly in American periodicals and have won Pushcart, O. Henry, and National Magazine awards. He lives in Copenhagen and teaches in the low-residency MFA Program of Fairleigh Dickinson University.

Steve Davenport is the author of a book of poems, *Uncontainable Noise* (2006), a couple of chapbooks, one of which was first listed as Notable in *Best American Essays* 2007, and a story that received a Special Mention in the 2011 *Pushcart Prize* anthology. Recent scholarship includes an essay about Richard Hugo's poetry in *All Our Stories Are Here: Critical Perspectives on Montana Literature* (University of Nebraska Press, 2009). A story received a Special Mention in the 2011 Pushcart Prize anthology.

Stephen Dunn is the author of 14 books of poetry. His collection *Different Hours* won the Pulitzer Prize in 2001. His collection, *Everything Else in the World,* was published in 2006. Among his other awards are three National Endowment for the Arts Creative Writing Fellowships, an Academy Award in Literature from The American Academy of Arts and Letters, and Fellowships from the Guggenheim and Rockefeller Foundations. His book, *Local Time*, was a winner of the National Poetry Series in 1986.

Steve Heller directs the MFA in Creative Writing Program at Antioch University

Los Angeles. Steve is the author of two published novels, *The Automotive History of Lucky Kellerman* (a Book-of-the-Month Club selection and QPB selection) and *Father's Mechanical Universe*, and a collection of short stories, *The Man Who Drank a Thousand Beers*. His short stories have earned many distinctions, including two O. Henry Awards. Steve's essays and creative nonfiction have appeared in numerous journals, including *Fourth Genre, Mānoa, New Letters, Colorado Review,* and *American Cowboy*. Steve is a regular reviewer for *Literary Magazine Review* and helped found two national literary journals, *Hawaii Review* and *Mid-American Review*. He is currently nearing completion of a new novel, *Return of the Ghost Killer*.

Sam Hamod was nominated for the Pulitzer Prize in poetry for *Dying With the Wrong Name*. He has published 10 books of poems; his latest is *Just Love Poems For You* (Ishmael Reed Pub/Contemporary Poetry Press, 2006). He has his Ph.D. and has taught at the Writers Workshop at the U. of Iowa, as well as at Princeton, Michigan, Wisconsin, Howard and other places. He has received numerous awards and fellowships; in addition, he was voted the outstanding Arab American poet by the Ethnic Heritage Society. He has also published work in a plethora of magazines and anthologies, among them *Settling America*, ed. D. Kherdian, *Unsettling America*, ed. Gillan & Gillan, and *From Totem to Hip Hop*, ed. Ishmael Reed.

Robert Gover's latest novel, *On the Run with Dick and Jane* was published in 2006 (Hopewell Publications). Written when he was 30, his novel, *One Hundred Dollar Misunderstanding*, became a best-seller. He won the "Most Unsung Writer in America" award at the PEN International Convention in 1985. He has published nine novels and two works of nonfiction.

Albert Goldbarth won his second National Book Critics Circle Award for poetry in 2002. He is the recipient of a Guggenheim Fellowship. He has published 43 books, including his latest collection, *Everyday People*, from Graywolf Press.

Walter Cummins has published more than one hundred stories, three story collections, two novels and numerous essays. He is editor-in-chief of *The Literary Review*. His latest story collection is *The End of the Circle* (Egress Books, 2010). Cummins is a core faculty member of the Fairleigh Dickinson University MFA program.

Jack Marshall has published twelve books of poetry, of which *Sesame*, 1993, was awarded the PEN Center West Award, a Pushcart Prize, and was a finalist for the National Book Critics Circle Award. Two other books, *Arriving on the Playing Fields of Paradise*, 1984, and *Gorgeous Chaos; New and Selected Poems,*

1965-2001, won a Bay Area Book Reviewers Award. A collection of new poems, *The Steel Veil*, was published by Coffee House Press in Fall, 2008. He has also published a memoir, *From Baghdad to Brooklyn; Growing Up in a Jewish-Arabic Family in Midcentury America*, from Coffee House Press, 2005, which was voted a finalist for the PEN Center Award in Creative Non-Fiction. In 2008 Marshall was awarded a Guggenheim. He lives in the San Francisco Bay Area.

Greg Herriges is a professor of English at William Rainey Harper College in Palatine, Illinois. He is the author of five books, *Someplace Safe* (St. Martin's Press/ Avon Paperbacks), *Secondary Attachments* (William Morrow), *The Winter Dance Party Murders* (Wordcraft of Oregon), *JD: A Memoir of a Time and a Journey* (Wordcraft of Oregon), and *Street Hearts*, a new ebook. His short works, both fiction and non-fiction, have appeared in *The Chicago Tribune Magazine*, *The Literary Review*, *The South Carolina Review*, *Story Quarterly*, and Great Britain's *Popular Music and Society*. He has recently contributed historical and critical articles to *The Encyclopedia of Beat Literature* (Facts on File), and has written and produced three documentary films—*Thomas E. Kennedy: Copenhagen Quartet*, and the award winning *Player: A Rock and Roll Dream*, and *T.C. Boyle: The Art of the Story*.

Steve Kowit is the author of 12 books of poetry and has published a popular guide to writing poetry: *In the Palm of Your Hand*. Kowit received a B.A. degree from Brooklyn College, a Master of Arts degree from San Francisco State College, and a Master of Fine Arts degree from Warren Wilson College. He teaches at Southwestern College in Chula Vista, California and lives near the Tecate Mexican border. His acclaimed collection, *The Gods of Rapture*, won the Ted Geisel Award for the best San Diego book of 2006. *The First Noble Truth* won the Tampa Review Prize and was published in 2007. Kowit has won two Pushcart Prizes and an NEA fellowship for his poetry.

David Poe lives in France with his wife and son, dividing his time between Paris and Normandy. His stories have appeared in *StoryQuarterly*, *The Literary Review*, *Prairie Schooner*, and *Cimarron Review*. All of his stories have been nominated for Pushcart Prizes and one was selected as among the best 100 mystery stories of the year.

Victor Rangel-Ribeiro was born in 1925 in Goa and grew up trilingual. After establishing himself as a writer in Bombay, he migrated to New York in 1956. There he covered concerts for *The New York Times*, became copy chief at an ad agency, ran a famous music antiquariat, was named music director at the Beethoven Society, taught in the city's public and private schools, and edited some forty book manuscripts for New York publishers. His books on classical music include translations from the French (twenty poems by Maeterlinck, Verlaine and others, set to music by Chausson) and the Italian (*Classical Bel Canto Technique*, by Mme. Damoreau, a mid-19th century opera star). In 1991 he won a New York Foundation for the Arts Fiction Fellowship, and in 1998 the Milkweed National Fiction Prize for his debut novel, *Tivolem*, which *Booklist* called one of the twenty notable first novels of the year. His short stories have appeared in the *Iowa, North American,* and *Literary Reviews* and in other publications here and in India. A short story collection, *Loving Ayesha*, was published by HarperCollins (India) in 2003. A member of American MENSA, he is currently on the international online creative writing faculty at Fairleigh Dickinson University. He has just completed his second novel, *The Fires of Gangapur*.

Lennox Raphael, a New Yorker Trinidadian, lives in Copenhagen, Denmark with his wife and daughter. A former staff writer for the *East Village Other* (EVO), his first play, *Che!*, ran for over a year in Manhattan; and he has written & directed *Blue Soap, Waiting for Mick Jaggger,* and several other works for the theater. Raphael has published five books of poetry. He is the co-author, with Maryanne Raphael, of *Garden of Hope,* a memoir, published by Hopewell in 2006. His work-in-progress is *Naipaul's Country*, a novel.

Nicholas Birns teaches at the New School in New York City. He is editor of *Antipodes* and Secretary-Treasurer of the Council of Editors of Learned Journals. His book *Understanding Anthony Powell* came out from the University of South Carolina Press in 2004, and his co-edited *Companion to Australian Literature Since 1900* appeared in 2007. His book *Theory After Theory* appeared from Broadview in 2010.

George Dickerson has been on the staff of *The New Yorker*, Managing Editor of *Cavalier*, Editor of *Story* and Contributing Editor of *Time*, Founding Editor-in Chief of *Rattapallax*, as well as Head of Press and Publications for UNRWA (United Nations Relief and Works Agency for Palestine Refugees in the Near East). Dickerson's poetry has appeared in *The New Yorker, Mademoiselle, Rattapallax, Nadada,* and *Medicinal Purposes, a Literary Review*. His *Selected Poems 1959-1999* (Rattapallax Press, 2000) includes his one-man drama *A Few Useless Mementos for Sale*, produced on stage in New York and Hollywood. He has won several poetry awards, including first prize in the international 1999 Lyric Recovery Award contest, second prize in the 2001 Marilyn K. Prescott Awards, and first prize in the 2001 *Medicinal Purposes, a Literary Review,* poetry contest. His short stories have appeared in *The Best American Short Stories of 1963* and *1966*. A professional actor since 1977, George has been on the New York stage and was featured in, or co-starred in, 20 feature films, including David Lynch's *Blue Velvet* (as Detective Williams) and James Foley's *After Dark, My Sweet* (as Doc Goldman). He has also guest-starred in 30 prime-time TV series and played the recurring role of Commander Swanson during the first season of *Hill Street Blues*. He is a member of the Academy of Motion Picture Arts and Sciences.

Paul Casey lives in the Pacific Northwest, where, in addition to his full-time job helping not-for-profits improve their websites, he is an adjunct faculty member at Washington State University in Vancouver, WA.

Liam Mac Sheóinín is a contributing and review editor for *The Irish Edition* and *Abiko Quarterly*. His first novel, *George W. Bush Buys Coke in Mid-Eternity*, was published by Serving House Books. His work has been nominated for the Pushcart Prize.

Joseph Millar's two collections are *Overtime* and *Fortune*, both from EWU Press. A third collection, *Blue Rust*, is due out in early 2012 from Carnegie-Mellon. He teaches in Pacific University's low-residency MFA program and lives in Raleigh, NC.

Michael S. Begnal has published four books of poetry. His first, *The Lakes of Coma*, appeared in 2003 from Six Gallery Press, followed in 2005 by the long poem *Mercury, the Dime*. His collection *Ancestor Worship* was published by Salmon Poetry in 2007, and his latest, *Future Blues*, appears from the same press in 2011. He was included in the anthologies *Breaking the Skin: New Irish Poetry* (Black Mountain Press, 2002), *Salmon: A Journey in Poetry* (Salmon, 2007), and in Irish Gaelic, *Go Nuige Seo* (Coiscéim). Begnal has appeared in numerous literary journals as well as in a collection of essays titled *Avant-Post: The Avant-Garde under "Post-" Conditions* (Litteraria Pragensia). He was formerly the editor of the Galway, Ireland-based literary magazine, *The Burning Bush*. At the age of 41, he earned an MFA from North Carolina State University.

Jack Driscoll is the author of three novels, a collection of short stories, and three books of poems. Winner of the AWP Short Fiction Award, his stories have appeared regularly in *The Georgia Review* and *The Southern Review*. He currently teaches in Pacific University's low-residency MFA program in Oregon. Driscoll's latest story collection, *The World of a Few Minutes Ago*, will be published by Wayne State University Press in spring 2012. The spring issue of *The Georgia Review* lists Driscoll in their Best Fiction of the Last Twenty Five Years. His essay about his fiction is currently on their website.www.uga.edu/garev/.

Mario Vargas Llosa, Peru's foremost writer, is the author of more than 30 books. He has written six plays and several volumes of literary essays including Making Waves, which won the National Book Critics Circle Award. He has won the Cervantes Prize, the Spanish-speaking world's most distinguished literary honor, and the Jerusalem Prize. In 2010 Mario Vargas Llosa was honored with the Nobel Prize for Literature.

Duff Brenna is Professor Emeritus at Cal-State University, San Marcos, where he was given three Outstanding Faculty Awards. He is an AWP Best Novel winner, and the recipient of an NEA Fellowship. His third novel, *Too Cool,* was a *New York Times* Noteworthy Book. His fourth novel, *The Altar of the Body*, was Book Editor's Favorite Book of the Year at *South Florida Sun-Sentinel*. His sixth novel, *The Law of Falling Bodies* (Hopewell Publications), was published September 2007.

Niels Hav is a full-time poet and short story writer living in Copenhagen with a number of awards from The Danish Arts Council. In English he has *We Are Here*, published by Book Thug, and poetry and fiction in numerous magazines including *The Literary Review*, *Shearsman*, and *PRISM International*. In his native Danish he is the author of six collections of poetry and three books of short fiction. His work has been translated into several languages such as Spanish, Arabic, Turkish and Chinese. He travels a lot, sometimes in the USA.

Acknowledgments

"Turning Fifty", from LANDSCAPE AT THE END OF THE CENTURY by Stephen Dunn. Copyright © 1991 by Stephen Dunn. Used by permission of W.W. Norton & Company, Inc.

"Sixty", from DIFFERENT HOURS by Stephen Dunn. Copyright © 2000 by Stephen Dunn. Used by permission of W.W. Norton & Company, Inc.

"I Am Joe's Prostate" by Thomas E. Kennedy appeared originally in *New Letters* magazine (2007) and was reprinted in *The Best American Magazine Writing* (2008) and in Danish in Euroman (2008) and the Danish P.E.N. anthology *Herfra min verden går* (2009).

Niels Hav's "Encouragement" first appeared in *We Are Here*, published by Book Thug Toronto (2006). Reprinted with permission.

Michael S. Begnal's poem "Shade" first appeared in *Notre Dame Review*, and "The Fluctuations" first appeared at Todd Swift's blog site, *Eyewear*.

"Badinage for 'Pepper'" Copyright © 2004, 2005 by George Dickerson first published in *Medicinal Purposes, a Literary Review,* Spring 2005; "El Gallo's Last Faena" Copyright © 1999, 2000 by George Dickerson in *George Dickerson Selected Poems 1959-1999*, Rattapallax Press, New York April 2000; "Toward Absolute Zero" Copyright © 1999, 2000 by George Dickerson first published in *Rattapallax*, No. 3, Spring 2000 and *George Dickerson Selected Poems 1959—1999*, Rattapallax Press, New York April 2000. (Note: It also won first prize in Philophonema's international Lyric Recovery Awards in 1999.)

Walter Cummins' "After Aging" was first published online in *The Conversation* at http://mals.retroforward.com/.

Mario Vargas Llosa's "Diabribe against the Sportsman" is excerpted from the novel, *The Notebooks of Don Rigoberto,* translated from the Spanish by Edith Grossman and published by Farrar, Strauss & Giroux in 1998.

Women Write about Aging

As a companion collection to *Winter Tales: Men Write About Aging*, Serving House Books will soon publish *Winter Tales: Women Write About Aging*.

The women's version promises to be every bit as entertaining and thought-provoking as the men's, encapsulating the thoughts of **Eleanor Roosevelt**, who famously said, "I could not, at any age, be content to take my place in a corner by the fireside and simply look on."

Some of the contributors include **Abby Frucht**, who writes about the aspect of self gained through the scars of inescapable loss; **Andi Olsen**'s photo art captures "Excessive Exposure to Time;" **Dorianne Laux**'s poetry illuminates how "the future shows up everywhere;" **Elisabeth Murawski**'s poems attempt to reconcile the internalized image of self "trapped in flesh that sags like yesterday's balloon;" **Laurie Stone** talks about embracing love and relocating her East Coast life to Phoenix, Arizona; and **Ursula K. Le Guin** discusses how long it takes to become "human."

While aging involves no small amount of trepidation, the women contributors of *Winter Tales* are no whiney sissies, choosing, instead, to explore the aging process through "a fragile dewdrop on its perilous way."

www.ingramcontent.com/pod-product-compliance
Lightning Source LLC
Chambersburg PA
CBHW020726210626
46807CB00016B/363